Praise for *Two Extra Steps*

"Prior to meeting Bill, I was focusing on 'top-line' revenue and trying to grow our Company's revenue as high as possible, and as fast as possible without even a consideration for profit. I thought the more revenue I generated the more profit we would increase and I was totally wrong.

With Bill's guidance, coaching, and techniques, we implemented new initiatives like automation, dynamic pricing, and watching our ROI on every marketing expense, but one of the biggest things I learned from Bill was to develop an intimate relationship with my financials which was non-existent previously.

Within a couple years our overall revenue decreased (mainly due to firing our largest Client) but our overall profit, as a percentage of overall sales, grew significantly and is now more than quadrupled since Bill started coaching me as we have found an untapped niche to penetrate and have put in the 2ExtraSteps for the last 5–6 years to see this growth.

Bill helped to show me how to become successful by showing me how to focus on the right things that will actually grow my business while eliminating what doesn't."

—Sam Rubin, Founder/CEO of Four Seasons Concierge

"Most people talk about excellence. Bill Faeth lives it. *Two Extra Steps* distills decades of hard-earned lessons into a practical framework that shows why success belongs to those willing to think differently and execute longer than everyone else. This book is not about hustle for hustle's sake. It is about standards, consistency, and doing the unglamorous work that compounds into extraordinary results. If you want a clear, proven path to stand out in business and life, this book delivers it."

– Dave Gambrill, Digital Marketing Mentorship

"There are educators, there are coaches, and then there are visionaries—men who don't just teach an industry but transform it. Bill Faeth is one of those rare forces of change. His wisdom, experience, and relentless passion don't just help people make money—they unlock generational wealth. This book and Bill's teachings aren't just lessons; they are a road map to a future most only dream of. Few walk this earth with the integrity, insight, and impact of Bill Faeth. A legendary entrepreneur, an extraordinary father, a devoted husband, and a friend whose influence will echo for years to come."

– Pace Morby, TV Host, Author, Investor, Entrepreneur, Speaker, and the GOAT of Creative Financing

"Bill has the rare talent of being both a brilliant real estate investor and one of the best educators in the industry. This book not only defies conventional wisdom, it gives a proven road map to break free from the rat race and build lasting wealth. Don't read this book unless you're serious about creating the life of your dreams!"

– Jerry Norton, Founder, Flipping Mastery

"Joining Bill Faeth's accelerator program in 2022 was one of the most impactful decisions I have ever made for building and growing my business. What began as a strategic investment quickly became a transformational experience. Bill's program didn't just help me scale my short-term rental business tenfold and beyond—it gave me a clear, proven blueprint to do it intentionally, sustainably, and in alignment with the life I wanted to build.

What resonated with me most was Bill's philosophy around growth. In an industry where success is often measured by door count and vanity metrics, Bill challenges that narrative. He asks a far more important question: What do you actually need to meet your goals? His belief in making the most money from the least amount of properties completely shifted my perspective. Instead of chasing scale for the sake of scale, I learned how to design a business that supports freedom, focus, and long-term fulfillment—without needing 100+ doors.

What truly sets Bill apart, however, goes far beyond short-term rentals. His mentorship extended into our life plan, our other business ventures, and our long-term vision. He didn't just coach the business—he coached the whole person. Even after major milestones were reached, Bill followed up to check in, see how things were going, and offer guidance where needed.

In a world where most influencers and leaders are inaccessible, Bill is different. Many times I sent what I thought would be a quick message, only to have Bill pick up the phone and call me directly. That level of care, presence, and authenticity is rare—and it's what separates Bill from others in our space.

I am deeply grateful for his mentorship, leadership, and genuine investment in my growth. His impact will be felt in my business and my life for years to come."

– Joe Rohne, Short Term Real Estate Realtor

Also by Bill Faeth

Super Properties:
Your Step-by-Step Guide to Making $250,000 Per Year from Airbnbs with One Up-Front Investment

TWO EXTRA STEPS

THE UNFAIR EDGE ANYONE CAN USE

BILL FAETH

Matt Holt Books
An Imprint of BenBella Books, Inc.
Dallas, TX

This book is designed to provide accurate and authoritative information about entrepreneurship. Neither the author nor the publisher is engaged in rendering legal, accounting, or other professional services by publishing this book. If any such assistance is required, the services of qualified professionals should be sought. The author and publisher will not be responsible for any liability, loss, or risk incurred as a result of the use and application of any information contained in this book.

Matt Holt is an imprint of BenBella Books, Inc.
8080 N. Central Expressway
Suite 1700
Dallas, TX 75206
benbellabooks.com
Send feedback to feedback@benbellabooks.com

BenBella and *Matt Holt* are federally registered trademarks.

Printed in the United States of America
10 9 8 7 6 5 4 3 2 1

Library of Congress Control Number: 2025050731
ISBN 9781637749166 (hardcover)
ISBN 9781637749173 (electronic)

Editing by Katie Dickman
Copyediting by Michael Fedison
Proofreading by Jenny Bridges and Denise Pangia
Text design and composition by Jordan Koluch
Cover design by Paul McCarthy
Printed by Versa Press

I would like to dedicate this to my two daughters
in hopes that they have learned the value of the Two Extra Steps
and to Earl & Tiger Woods for teaching this to me subconsciously.

Contents

Chapter 1

THE DEATH OF AVERAGE

Exhausted and drenched in sweat, I stepped off the 18th green at El Dorado Golf Course in Long Beach, California. It was July 1989. One of those brutally hot Southern California summer days, probably 110 degrees. I was 16 years old, finishing my first major junior championship. And not just any tournament. This was the Long Beach Junior Match Play Championship, one of the most competitive events in the state.

I had just shot my first under-par round in a major. Seventy-one. One under.

I remember sitting at the scoring table, heart pounding, hands trembling as I double-checked my scorecard. My fingers struggled to add up the numbers—threes, fours, fives—as I checked my card and verified each hole. I'd never had that much trouble with single digits in my life. But there it was. A 71. When I looked up at the leaderboard, my name was the only one in red. The only score under par. I was leading.

For a teenager, it was pure euphoria. I had worked for years to reach this moment. Nearly 200 kids were competing that day—one round, one shot to qualify for match play. Legends like Fred Couples and Phil Mickelson had played in this same event. This was *the* tournament in Southern California junior golf. And my name was at the top of the leaderboard.

It wasn't the Masters, but to me, it might as well have been.

As I signed my card, my mom came out from the pro shop. She hadn't walked the course. She couldn't. Too nervous to watch, she'd been inside chain-smoking Marlboro Menthols all morning, probably burning through two packs. I imagined her ashtray looked like a volcano. But when she walked up to me, eyes wide, proud and relieved, it was one of the happiest moments of both our lives. I will never forget her smell, her hug, or the look in her eyes. That was *our* win.

And then everything changed.

I turned back toward the green to watch the next group finish. One of the kids walking up was a friend of mine. Scrawny. Three years younger than me. He collapsed just short of the green from heat exhaustion. But after what felt like forever, maybe a minute, he did it. He got back up, dropped his bag, lined up his putt, and drained it. Ten, maybe 12 feet. That was the first time I saw it: the fist pump.

That kid was Eldrick Woods. You know him now as Tiger.

His dad, Earl, rushed out, scooped him up, and carried him to the scorer's table. Tiger had just shot a 64. Seven strokes better than me after collapsing from heat exhaustion. It was superhuman. Or, at least, that's what it looked like on the surface.

I was still proud of what I had done, but that exhilarated feeling? It vanished. Just like that. The best round I had ever played wasn't even close to what he had just done.

Most people would chalk it up to raw talent. And yeah, Tiger had more talent in his 13-year-old swing than I could dream of. But that day taught me something important: Talent wasn't the separator. Because the real difference between him and everyone else wasn't just on the leaderboard. It was in what happened next.

THE LESSON THAT CHANGED EVERYTHING

We all sat down in the clubhouse for lunch. Me, my mom, Earl, and Tiger. We hadn't even ordered before Earl started drilling him. I didn't say a word. Neither did my mom. Neither did Tiger. We just listened. Earl Woods wasn't congratulating his son. He was coaching him. Sharpening him. That lunch wasn't a celebration. It was a clinic.

"What were you thinking on the third hole? What was your mindset? Were you visualizing your approach shots or thinking three ahead?"

It wasn't scolding. It was precision. Earl wasn't replaying the 64 Tiger just shot. He was preparing him for the next one.

"One shot at a time," he repeated. "You give 120% in the 30 seconds before every shot. Not 110. Not 105. One hundred twenty."

After lunch, they didn't go home. They went to the range. For nearly two more hours, Tiger hit balls while Earl corrected what he saw as two flaws in an otherwise perfect round. Then came the bunker. Then the putting green. Tiger had missed one short putt that day, so now it was 300 five-footers in a row.

Let that sink in: The kid had just outperformed nearly 200 golfers—including me—in brutal conditions. Seven strokes better than my best day ever. Most people would have celebrated, bragged, and taken the afternoon off. Not Tiger. His day wasn't over, because greatness doesn't clock out when the round ends. It doubles down.

That was the difference. And that's when it clicked for me.

Growing up without a father, I think I latched onto Earl that day without even realizing it. The way he coached Tiger, the expectations he set, the balance of intensity and care—something in me recognized what I was missing. That guiding light. That push to be more.

Even now, decades later, I can still hear Earl's voice. I still remember the way he carried himself. The way he carried Tiger. He was tough, but not cruel. Stern, but never detached. He made Tiger better because he expected more from him. And most of all, he modeled what it looked like to demand more than "good enough."

That day was when I started to understand that greatness doesn't belong to the smartest or even the most talented. It belongs to the ones who think like others don't and are willing to do what others won't. And Tiger did. I watched it happen.

He thought differently. He prepared differently. He acted differently. That mindset and the actions that followed are why his name is etched into history.

I knew then that if I wanted to become great, I'd have to find a way to replicate that discipline, that expectation, and that follow-through.

OUTWORKING EVERYONE

A few months later, when my grandfather came to visit, he saw I was serious about golf. He wasn't Earl, but he stepped in in his own way—softer, more encouraging—and gave me something I'd never really had: The gift of expectation. Of being seen as someone with potential and being held to it.

The problem? He couldn't be there every day. And I knew it. He could visit. He could check in. He could believe in me. But if I was going to be great, the drive had to come from me. I would have to set my own standards and hold myself accountable to them.

We didn't have money, but my mom, a schoolteacher, scraped together enough for a membership at Sundale Country Club. It wasn't fancy. But it was mine and I treated it like it was Augusta.

So, I started showing up before school. Guys like my friend Rob Thompson had more natural ability. But I was the one hitting five-footers in the dark before homeroom. The one back on the range before the team even showed up for practice. The one spending every free minute trying to re-create what I saw that day at El Dorado. Grinding. Repeating. Failing. Repeating again.

I wasn't the most talented golfer in Bakersfield. Not even close. But I outworked everyone else. Not just because I wanted to win, but because I understood what winning required.

That's where I built my unfair edge. Where I separated myself from the pack. Not with talent. With focus, time, and effort.

And then, it paid off. All the five-footers in the dark, the mornings before school, the grind nobody saw—it led to something big. I earned a full-ride scholarship to UCLA. For a kid from Bakersfield, that was the dream. It felt like I'd made it.

Or so I thought.

Chapter 2

THE TWO EXTRA STEPS

The scholarship to UCLA should've been the moment everything clicked. Instead, it became the moment everything crashed. One year later, I was a college dropout. And as crazy as it sounds, that failure became the foundation for everything that followed. Yep, the kid who earned a full-ride scholarship to UCLA—one of the most prestigious golf programs in the country—walked away.

Since then, I've built 39 businesses, exited multiple times, and generated over a billion dollars in lifetime sales. I've done it all: launched e-commerce brands, run restaurants, built software companies, created glow-in-the-dark mini golf, scaled marketing agencies, and operated multimillion-dollar ground transport companies.

I've hosted sold-out conferences with thousands of attendees, coached some of the biggest names you can imagine, and today I run Build STR Wealth—the #1 education platform in the short-term rental industry. I own a real estate portfolio worth $23 million and growing, which started with a single, calculated investment of $126,000.

Why am I telling you this?

Because none of what I've built happened by accident. It wasn't luck.

It wasn't because I had better connections or a fancy degree. It wasn't from deep pockets or raw talent.

I got here because I made decisions most people won't make. Then I committed to doing the things other people avoid. I call it the **Two Extra Steps**.

That's what this book is about: **thinking like others don't and doing what others won't**. The people who win in business (and life) are the ones who take the **Two Extra Steps** that seem small on the surface, but create massive separation over time.

Every story, every strategy you'll read ties back to those Two Extra Steps because that's your unfair edge over your competitors. If you're an entrepreneur, a business owner, or just someone who refuses to settle for average, this is your competitive playbook.

WHAT ARE THE TWO EXTRA STEPS?

There's a reason I started this book with a golf story. What I witnessed that day—Tiger Woods collapsing from heat exhaustion, then shooting 64, then heading straight to the range while everyone else went home—wasn't just talent on display. It was something deeper.

Tiger thought differently. Then he acted differently. That combination is what created separation. It's what transformed a 13-year-old kid into the most dominant golfer in history.

That pattern is also the same one I've built every business around for the last 30 years: *Think like others don't. Do what others won't.*

Here's what the **Two Extra Steps** are.

STEP ONE: THINK WHAT OTHERS DON'T

Before you can out-execute your competition, you have to outthink them. Most people believe their edge will come from doing more. Longer hours, more hustle, more grind. But what it really comes down to is this:

You can't outwork someone who outthinks you.

This is where separation begins—long before anyone sees the scoreboard. It shows up in how you think. How you decide. How you hold yourself accountable when no one's watching.

Most people obsess over the outer game. Strategies, hacks, and shortcuts. But if you want to build something that lasts, you start here: clarity, standards, and the mindset to sustain both.

Once your thinking shifts, your actions follow.

1. Lead with Clarity and Vision

- Get clear on where you're going—and why it matters.
- Strip away distractions so you can double down on what moves the needle.
- Look beyond the obvious. See the angles and opportunities others ignore.
- Question every assumption—even the ones you've held for years.

2. Set Your Standards

- Stop accepting "good enough" as the finish line.
- Define the minimums you'll never compromise on.
- Treat everything you do like it matters—because it does.
- Think like a professional, not a hobbyist.

3. Play the Long Game

- Think in years and decades, not days and weeks.
- Build strategy around future positioning, not just short-term wins.
- Sacrifice convenience now for leverage later.

Bottom line: This is the operating system shift. When you think like this, your next move isn't a reaction—it's a strategy. You aren't playing the same game as everyone else. You're building the advantage before the competition even sees it coming.

STEP TWO: DO WHAT OTHERS WON'T

Here's where most people fail. They understand the concept. They like the idea. But when it costs extra time, extra effort, or extra money . . . they stop. Most people fall off here not because it's hard, but because it's repetitive. Excellence is built in the monotony. It's the reps, the boring work, the daily discipline that compounds into something extraordinary.

1. Go All In

- Go all in where others hesitate.
- Invest time, money, and energy most people avoid.
- Act decisively instead of overthinking.
- Eliminate busy work. Move on what matters.

2. Out-Execute Everyone

- Consistently do the work others avoid.
- Finish strong when others settle for good enough.
- Show up when motivation dies.
- Make persistence your default setting.

3. Raise the Bar

- Make excellence your minimum, not your maximum.
- Do it when no one's watching—especially then.
- Redefine what excellence looks like in your market.

Bottom line: Where most people check the box and clock out, you double down. That's the difference between good and great.

When you commit to thinking differently and acting differently, three things happen:

- Your competitors can't keep up—not because they lack talent, but because they lack willingness.
- Your customers feel the difference—even if they can't explain it.
- Your business compounds because your habits compound.

This is the foundation for everything that follows. Thinking differently and acting differently gives you the edge, but only if you're headed in the right direction.

The biggest mistake I see entrepreneurs make? They start building without knowing who they're building for. And when you skip that step, every decision—pricing, branding, marketing—becomes guesswork.

That's why the next chapter starts with the most important question in business.

Chapter 3

DEFINING YOUR BUYER PERSONA

Most businesses start with the wrong question: "How do I sell more of what I have?" That's backward. The right question is this: "Who exactly am I building this for and what do they really want?"

Because if you don't know that, everything else becomes guesswork. Your marketing. Your pricing. Your product road map. Even your operations.

You're not selling a product. You're solving a problem for a specific person. The clearer you are about who that person is, the faster everything else clicks.

WHERE MOST BUSINESSES GO WRONG

Most entrepreneurs never go far enough. They assume they know. They tell themselves they are selling to "busy moms," "small business owners," or "people who love fitness." That is not a buyer persona. That is a vague category.

A real buyer persona isn't a label. It's a person you know so well you can describe their habits, their routines, their favorite brands, what stresses them out, how they justify spending money, where they hang out online, and how they make decisions—emotionally, logically, impulsively, or cautiously.

Without this level of clarity, everything downstream becomes harder.

- **Product development** becomes a gamble.
- **Pricing** feels like a shot in the dark.
- **Marketing** becomes expensive and ineffective.
- **Sales** become unpredictable.
- **Customer retention** becomes an uphill climb.

You end up guessing at what people want, hoping you stumble into sales. Sometimes you get lucky. Most of the time, you don't.

But when you do get it right—when you fully understand who you are building for before you build it—everything changes. Products fit better. Messaging resonates better. Pricing holds without pushback. Marketing converts cheaper. Customer retention skyrockets.

You're no longer selling to everyone. You're selling to the right someone.

HOW WE GOT IT WRONG—AND FIXED IT

When my wife and I opened Wild Bill's Texas Smokehouse in Taft, California, we made the same mistake that derails so many entrepreneurs: We built the business for ourselves. We built what we loved. We created the menu we wanted to eat. We designed the restaurant around our vision of great barbecue. We chose the layout, the recipes, the meats, the sides—all based on what we enjoyed, what we had learned, and what excited us personally.

And to be fair, the food itself was excellent. I had done the work. I had flown to Texas, traveled city to city, and studied under one of the best pitmasters I could find. I brought back world-class recipes. The meats were smoked to perfection. The sides were made from scratch. The quality wasn't the problem. In fact, the quality is what gave us confidence to open in the first place.

But a great product doesn't automatically create a great business.

The problem was who we were targeting. Or, more accurately, who we weren't.

We assumed "anyone who's hungry" was our customer. That's not a buyer persona. That's a wish. And wishes don't build profitable businesses.

While the locals enjoyed the food, there simply weren't enough people in the small town to support a fast-casual walk-in barbecue restaurant at scale. Our model was essentially Chipotle-style service: Customers would walk in, choose their meats, pick their sides, sit down, and eat. For a while, it worked well enough during the busy lunch hour. But by dinner, traffic dropped off. On weekends, it slowed even more. We weren't McDonald's. We didn't have mass volume like they did, but we were trying to run the business like they did.

It wasn't until we zoomed out and really studied the market that the real opportunity became clear. Taft wasn't just a small town . . . it was a small town surrounded by oil leases. Every weekday, workers from multiple oil fields would flood into town. While the town's residential population hovered around 15,000 to 20,000, the daytime population during the workweek ballooned to nearly 80,000 people.

These weren't families looking for a long, sit-down dinner. They were guys on tight lunch breaks who needed speed, consistency, and calories—fast. Something they could trust to be ready when they were.

But there was another layer we hadn't initially seen: the oil companies themselves. Beyond daily lunch breaks, these companies regularly hosted meetings, leadership summits, golf outings, and corporate events. Dozens, sometimes hundreds, of people gathered for catered meals. And almost nobody in town was serving that need.

That's when it clicked.

We didn't need to change the food. The food was already great. What we needed was to redesign the business model to serve these specific buyers. We optimized the ordering process to serve workers in five to seven minutes so they could be in and out before their lunch breaks ended. We created catering packages designed for large group orders. We adapted our prep schedules to smoke meats overnight and stage bulk orders for next-day deliveries. And we invested in the logistics to deliver directly to oil leases and jobsites, which was something nobody else in town was doing.

That pivot changed everything.

Within a few short months, catering became nearly 70% of our revenue. What started as a small-town BBQ restaurant transformed into a high-volume catering operation serving not just oil companies, but also weddings, corporate events, private parties, and community gatherings across the entire region. Eighteen months after making that shift, we exited the business successfully.

The food didn't make us profitable. Getting crystal clear on the **buyer persona** did.

THE MOST COMMON MISTAKES WHEN BUILDING BUYER PERSONA

Getting this wrong isn't always about being lazy. In fact, most business owners I work with are extremely hardworking. The problem is they are often working hard on the wrong things because they skipped this part entirely or made one of the following common mistakes.

Mistake 1: Building for Themselves

They build what excites them personally, assuming that if they like it, others will too. They fall in love with their own taste and preferences, not realizing their customer may think differently.

Mistake 2: Trying to Serve Everyone

They cast the widest net possible, thinking more potential customers = more sales. Instead, they end up with vague offers that resonate with no one.

Mistake 3: Starting with Features Instead of Problems

They focus on what their product does instead of why anyone should care. Great businesses start by obsessing over their customer's problem, not the feature list.

Mistake 4: Staying Surface-Level

They know demographics but not psychographics. They know their customer's age, income, and location but not their fears, frustrations, buying psychology, or emotional triggers.

Mistake 5: Believing Marketing Can Cover It

When sales stall, they assume they need more ads, more content, more marketing. But you can't out-market a weak product-to-buyer fit. Great marketing amplifies clarity. It can't create it.

BEYOND DEMOGRAPHICS: CREATING A REAL PERSON

This is where most people mail it in and don't take the Two Extra Steps. They stop at age, gender, income level, or job title and assume that's enough. It's not. Your ideal buyer persona needs to feel like a real person. Someone you could describe in conversation as if you've known them for years.

If you want to win, this is how you take the Two Extra Steps. You need to give them a name, a face, and a full personality profile. You should know:

What they drink

- Do they grab a craft IPA, a glass of Cabernet, a $20 bottle of bourbon, or sparkling water?

- Are they into kombucha and organic juices, or Diet Coke and Monster Energy drinks?
- This speaks to both **lifestyle and price sensitivity**.

What they drive

- Are they in a Toyota Camry because they value reliability?
- A Ford F-150 because they love utility and strength?
- A Mercedes or Tesla because image and status matter?
- This tells you whether they're buying **functionality, identity, or luxury.**

Where they live

- Do they own a home in the suburbs with a backyard?
- Rent an apartment downtown because they crave convenience?
- Or live in a rural cabin because they value independence and nature?
- Where someone lives reveals priorities: **space**, **location**, **access**, **or prestige**.

What they read

- Business books like *Atomic Habits* or *The 7 Habits of Highly Effective People*?
- Self-improvement blogs, fashion magazines, or tech articles?
- Or do they primarily consume social media captions and memes?
- This tells you **how they learn and what they aspire to**.

What they watch

- Netflix binge sessions or curated YouTube playlists?
- TikTok trends or old-school cable news?
- Completely unplugged because they value minimalism and productivity?
- Their media habits reveal **attention span, values, and social influence**.

If they watch Netflix

- True crime? They're curious, analytical.
- Documentaries? They value education and depth.
- Reality TV? They crave entertainment and escape.
- Sitcoms? They seek comfort and humor.
- This uncovers **emotional triggers** for your marketing.

What hobbies fill their weekends

- Are they hiking and biking? They value adventure and wellness.
- Playing golf or tennis? They value status, networking, and tradition.
- Gaming? They love competition and community—but on their terms.
- Hosting dinner parties? They crave connection and presentation.
- This helps you understand **what your product needs to complement or compete with**.

What values shape their financial decisions

- Do they prioritize security and stability, or experiences and adventure?
- Are they driven by **status, savings, or self-improvement**?
- Do they spend impulsively or cautiously?
- This directly informs **pricing and positioning**.

Where they spend their time online

- Are they living on Instagram, LinkedIn, Reddit, Pinterest, or niche Facebook groups?
- Do they scroll TikTok before bed or read long-form blogs on Substack?
- Knowing this lets you **meet them where they already are**.

What brands they trust

- Apple because they value simplicity and design.
- YETI because they value durability and prestige outdoors.

- Louis Vuitton because exclusivity matters.
- Walmart because price beats everything else.
- These brand affiliations reveal **psychological anchors for pricing and identity**.

What they secretly fear

- Looking incompetent at work.
- Missing out on trends (FOMO).
- Losing money.
- Wasting time on something that doesn't work.
- Fear is a buying motivator—**remove it and you win**.

What makes them proud

- Is it professional achievements?
- Owning luxury items and signaling success?
- Providing for their family?
- Traveling and collecting experiences?

The more layers of depth you add, the easier every future business decision becomes. Because you're no longer guessing. You're not trying to sell your product to "everyone with money." You're designing for someone who feels real. You're building for someone specific who will look at your offer and immediately recognize: "This was built for me."

SHAPE YOUR PRODUCT TO FIT YOUR BUYER

Once you know exactly who your ideal buyer is, your job is no longer to simply create a great product. Your job is to create a product that fits them so precisely it feels custom-built. This isn't about stacking up the most features or adding the fanciest packaging. It's about solving the exact problems your buyer wants solved, in the exact way they want them solved.

This is where real differentiation happens. You are not chasing what your competitors are doing. You are not copying what worked for someone else. You are building a solution that your buyer cannot ignore. It becomes so attractive and so clearly aligned with their needs that buying from you feels obvious. This is how you make your product feel irresistible to the person it was designed for.

When you get this right, you create pricing power. You do not need to compete by undercutting others. You can serve fewer people at a higher margin, which creates better profitability, more freedom, and more control over your business. Your buyer values the fit. They are not shopping for the cheapest option. They are looking for the solution that feels like it was built for them.

But this only works if you are willing to get specific. It only works if you are willing to fully understand your ideal buyer at the deepest level. You can't shape your product if you do not first know who you are shaping it for.

THE VIRAL PRODUCT PHENOMENON

You've seen it happen. A product hits the market and suddenly everyone wants it. The item itself isn't always revolutionary—it might be a toy, a sneaker drop, a subscription box. But the positioning and design speak so directly to what the buyer wants that demand becomes unstoppable.

That's not luck. That's alignment. It's the result of designing a product around the psychology of its ideal buyer. When you get that right, you stop chasing sales—and sales start chasing you.

Let's look at a real-world example.

EXAMPLE: WHO WOULD PAY $2,000 FOR WINE?

Not long ago, my wife and I were at our property in Montana. It was about 18 degrees outside. We had the firepit going, bundled up under blankets, and decided to open a bottle of Screaming Eagle Cabernet—a Christmas gift from my wife.

If you don't know wine, here's what you need to know: That bottle retails for over **$2,000**.

This isn't something we do often. It's not an everyday bottle for us. But that wine is a perfect example of what happens when a business knows exactly who its buyer is and builds the entire experience around serving them.

Screaming Eagle produces about 800 cases a year. That's fewer than 10,000 bottles. They could easily make 10 times that amount. They don't. The scarcity is intentional. The exclusivity isn't an accident—it's the product.

Their buyer isn't someone scanning the wine aisle at the grocery store. Their buyer is someone who values rarity, reputation, and the feeling of being part of an exclusive circle.

For that buyer, $2,000 isn't about the wine. It's about the story, the access, and the identity that comes with drinking something almost nobody else can. It's ego. It's emotion. And Screaming Eagle knows exactly how to deliver that.

For me? I'm not that buyer. I'm a value-driven buyer. Most nights, my wife and I are perfectly happy with a $40 bottle of Battalion red. Great wine, great experience, no guilt. For me, $2,000 feels excessive. For their buyer, $2,000 feels justified.

That's the point: Different buyers have different motivations, different price tolerances, and different definitions of value. And they need different products intentionally designed for them.

This is where so many entrepreneurs get it wrong. They build what excites *them* instead of asking the real questions:

- Who is my ideal buyer?
- What do they value most?
- What are they really paying for?

Screaming Eagle knows. That's why they can command $2,000 a bottle. If they scaled up to mass production, they'd kill the very thing that makes their wine desirable.

Exclusivity is the business model.

Your business works the same way. Before you worry about ads, funnels, or scaling, you start here. Figure out who your buyer is.

TWO EXTRA STEPS IN ACTION

While your competition:

- Settles for vague categories like "busy moms" or "business owners"
- Builds products for themselves instead of the customer
- Assumes "everyone" is their buyer and ends up resonating with no one
- Sells features and functions

You will:

- Get crystal clear on who your ideal buyer really is
- Uncover the values, triggers, and motivations behind their decisions
- Create products that feel tailor-made for one person—not the masses
- Build solutions so aligned they feel like the obvious choice
- Focus on delivering results your buyer cares about—not just features

The most profitable shift in your business won't come from complexity. It comes from the Two Extra Steps—knowing exactly who you're building for and aligning everything around them.

Chapter 4

WHY SATURATION IS YOUR OPPORTUNITY, NOT YOUR PROBLEM

Everywhere you look, markets feel crowded. Almost every product category is filled with competitors. Almost every service business has dozens—if not hundreds—of providers all offering something similar.

That's not a reason to panic. That doesn't mean you can't win. It's proof of opportunity. Crowded markets exist because there's demand. People are buying. The problem isn't the competition. The problem is when you don't differentiate yourself from the competition. You can't blend in. You need to be distinct. You need to give people a reason to choose you.

But this is where most entrepreneurs fail: They assume the only way to win is to have the best product or spend the most on marketing. Neither is true. You don't win by being slightly better at everything. You win by being intentionally different at one thing that matters. That's where the

Two Extra Steps come in: **Step 1: Think what others don't. Step 2: Do what others won't.**

While everyone else blends into the noise, you'll separate by design. Not by reinventing the wheel. Not by launching something the world has never seen. But by doing something your competitors won't—building a business so distinctive that your customer remembers you, chooses you, and keeps coming back.

Because saturation doesn't just punish the average business. It destroys it. And the difference between average and unforgettable often comes down to one thing: **the courage to take Two Extra Steps when everyone else stops at good enough**.

Maybe that reason is how your techs show up at the door. Maybe it's a pricing structure that's easier to understand and more valuable over time. Maybe it's the way your team treats people like real human beings instead of just service calls. It could be any of those things. What matters is that it's intentional.

Most companies struggle because they sit right in the middle. Not terrible. Not great. Just . . . there. They exist, but they don't lead. They serve customers, but don't build loyalty. They stay busy-ish, but don't scale profitably.

The businesses that break through aren't always bigger, smarter, or luckier. They just approach the same market with more clarity. They're intentional about who they serve, how they serve them, and what they're willing to do that others aren't.

WHY BIG COMPANIES FAIL AND SMALL COMPANIES WIN

You see it happen every single day. The giants fall asleep. The big companies, the brands that dominated for decades, get lazy. They get fat. They stop listening to their customers because they think they've already figured it out. They believe their size protects them.

And that's exactly how they get passed.

They don't get knocked out overnight. They get chipped away, little by little, by smaller companies who are willing to do what they won't. The companies who are still hungry. The ones who understand that if they keep taking the Two Extra Steps, they can carve off piece after piece of their competition's business.

That's the game.

The big companies stop innovating. They stop improving. They protect what they've built instead of asking where they're falling short. Meanwhile, here comes the smaller competitor—watching, listening, testing, iterating faster, solving problems the big guys either don't see or don't want to admit exist.

That's how a local shop becomes 5 locations. Then 10. Then 20. Because once you create separation, and you keep applying those Two Extra Steps consistently, you move into a category of one.

I've lived this firsthand. I've done it in my own companies over and over again.

The truth is, small companies aren't at a disadvantage. Not at all. They actually have the advantage because they can stay close to the customer. They can adapt faster. They can solve problems the big guys don't even realize are problems yet.

The big companies fall in love with the way they've always done it. The small companies fall in love with what the customer actually wants next.

And that's why they win. They pick a lane and stick to it.

THE THREE-LANE BUSINESS PHILOSOPHY

Business is a lot like driving on the freeway. You've got three choices: slow lane, middle lane, or fast lane. And the choice you make determines how far and how fast you go.

Most people? They merge into the middle. Because it feels safe. It feels comfortable. You're moving faster than the slow lane, but you're not pushing as hard as the fast lane. You're surrounded by other people doing the exact same thing, and you think, *I'm good. I'm keeping up.*

But the truth is the middle lane is the most dangerous lane on the road. You think you're safe because you're not crawling with the laggards in the slow lane, but you're not leading either. You're boxed in. You're reactive. You're playing defense while someone in the fast lane blows right by you.

In business, the middle lane looks like this:

- Trying to be good at everything and great at nothing
- Copying industry standards instead of creating your own
- Saying, "*We're competitive*," but never being memorable
- Busy enough to survive, but not distinctive enough to scale profitably

You know who lives in the middle lane? Sears. Kmart. Bed Bath & Beyond. They weren't terrible businesses. They weren't run by idiots. They were household names. They had decades of dominance. At one point, they were untouchable.

But then they got comfortable. They kept doing what had worked before, while the market shifted right under their feet. They told themselves they were "good enough." They stopped moving forward, and the companies willing to push into the fast lane passed them, then ran them off the road.

Now, let's talk about the slow lane for a second. The slow lane is the commodity game. Competing on price. Chasing low-margin scraps. Living in a race to the bottom. That lane will grind you into the pavement because there's always someone willing to do it cheaper.

The fast lane? That's where winners play. Not because they have the best product or the biggest budget, but because they made a choice. They said:

- We're not going to be average.
- We're not going to sit in traffic with everyone else.
- We're going to dominate ONE thing and do it at a level nobody else is willing to touch.

That's what gets you separation. That's what creates momentum. And once you build momentum in the fast lane, you don't just pass the competition . . . you leave them choking on dust.

What you can't afford to be is average. Remember this: **Average is death.** Ask Sears. Ask Kmart. Ask Bed Bath & Beyond. You can't. They're gone.

So what separated Amazon from those middle-lane giants? It wasn't just being online. It was how they approached the customer. Jeff Bezos built a model obsessed with convenience.

- Prime made delivery faster than anyone thought possible.
- One-click ordering eliminated friction completely.
- A $99 subscription didn't just buy shipping—it bought loyalty.

Amazon didn't win by selling books. They won by building an experience nobody else was willing to deliver. That's the fast-lane move. And everyone else? They're still stuck in traffic.

So ask yourself: Where are you right now? Slow lane? Middle lane? Or fast lane? And more importantly—where do you want to be?

And this is where most business owners start hedging:

"Sure, I'd love to be in the fast lane, but I don't have the biggest budget."

"I can't compete with those big brands."

"I don't have the best product in the market."

None of that matters. The fast lane isn't about having the best product or the deepest pockets. It's about taking the Two Extra Steps.

YOU DON'T NEED THE BEST PRODUCT TO WIN

People assume winning requires having the "best" product. It doesn't. Steve Jobs proved that with Apple. Now some might say Apple wins because it makes the *best* tech. But you could make a strong case that it doesn't.

PCs outperform Macs in raw computing power for the price. Android phones often launch with better cameras, faster charging, and more customization years before Apple adopts those features. And Apple is rarely first to market with new technology. They didn't invent MP3 players. They didn't invent smartphones. They didn't invent tablets or wireless earbuds.

So why do they dominate? Because they stopped playing the "feature war" game everyone else obsesses over. Apple didn't win on specs. They won on experience. They focused on three things competitors ignored . . .

1. **Marketing That Created a Cult Following**

   Apple positioned itself as the choice for people who "think different." It wasn't just tech—it was identity.
2. **Ease of Use**

   Their promise was simple: *It just works.* No manuals. No headaches. Just intuitive, seamless experience.
3. **Design That Made Tech Sexy**

   Sleek. Minimal. Beautiful. Apple products looked as good as they performed—something the industry had ignored.

That's the fast-lane move. While everyone else crammed in more features, Apple stripped out friction and turned functionality into a lifestyle. They didn't need the best product on paper. They nailed those three and suddenly the product isn't just a tool. It's a status symbol. That's why Apple can charge more than anyone else. That's why they created an ecosystem that locks people in for life.

Microsoft couldn't do it. Dell couldn't do it. Jobs turned functionality into a lifestyle and dominated the fast lane by thinking how others didn't and doing what others wouldn't.

IN-N-OUT BURGER: SIMPLICITY WINS

Now let's shift from tech to burgers. If anyone proves you don't need complexity to dominate, it's In-N-Out Burger.

While other fast-food chains fight to expand menus and add gimmicks, In-N-Out took the opposite approach: Do one thing, and do it flawlessly.

- Fresh, never-frozen beef.
- Fries cut in-house every day.
- A stripped-down menu: burgers, fries, shakes. That's it.

They could have chased Whataburger and Sonic with endless combos and "limited-time" specials. They didn't. They built a reputation for quality and consistency so strong that people will drive 30 miles out of their way for it.

And it wasn't just the food. In-N-Out layered in another fast-lane advantage: culture. In-N-Out pays employees more than competitors. They invest in training. They treat people with dignity in an industry notorious for churning through low-paid staff. That translates into something customers feel every time they pull up to the window: friendly, fast, professional service.

And then there's the layer most companies would never think to include: faith. Look closely at your cup or burger wrapper and you'll see Bible verses printed in tiny letters. It's not in-your-face marketing. It's their identity. It signals who they are and what they stand for. Combine that with being family-owned in a sea of corporate giants, and suddenly eating there feels like joining a community, not just grabbing fast food.

The result? People don't just eat In-N-Out—they evangelize it. They wear the merch like it's a fashion brand. They share the "secret menu" like an insider tip. They post photos of their meals as if it's an experience worth documenting.

This is how you stand out in a saturated category. Not by adding more. Not by racing to the bottom on price. By picking a lane—freshness, speed, culture—and owning it so completely that nobody else can keep up.

HOW TO STAND OUT IN A COMMODITY BUSINESS

You might be thinking, *That's great for burgers, but I run an HVAC company. How do I stand out when my industry is boring and price-driven?*

The answer? The exact same way. You do something nobody else is willing to do.

It could be customer service. It could be branding. It could be creating an experience that shocks and delights. Even something as simple as the way your techs show up at the door can set you apart.

Imagine this: You call an HVAC company and the tech shows up in a tuxedo to fix your AC. Would you remember that? Absolutely. You'd probably snap a photo. Post it online. Tell your friends. That one move turns an ordinary service call into a story. And stories create free marketing.

Because standing out isn't about adding more features. It's about creating moments customers talk about and never forget. The same principle applies on a bigger scale. When my business partner, Reg Boothe, and I launched Glow Golf—the first glow-in-the-dark miniature golf experience inside shopping malls—we didn't just start a business; we created an entirely new category.

THE GLOW GOLF INNOVATION: CREATING A NEW CATEGORY

While competitors were investing millions in massive outdoor fun centers, we went the opposite direction to create our Glow Golf experience. We went indoors where we could control the climate, the lighting, and the entire experience. Even more important, we placed our courses inside shopping malls, where built-in foot traffic gave us a steady stream of potential customers.

We did it faster. We did it easier and we went after volume. Our focus wasn't on building the most high-end course on the planet. It was about accessibility, speed, and scale. We wanted a model we could replicate quickly and dominate the space before anyone else saw the opportunity.

Here's what's crazy: We never ran television ads. Never bought radio spots. Never sent a single piece of direct mail. We didn't need to. Why? Because the product did the marketing for us.

We literally just built something super attractive, super new, super unique, most importantly, that people would walk by and say, "Oh my God, I've never seen anything like that before."

They tried it. They loved it. And then they told everyone they knew. That word of mouth fueled explosive growth.

It was the same principle Steve Jobs mastered at Apple, applied in a completely different industry: Create an experience so unique and so desirable that your customers become your loudest marketers. That's exactly what we did and it worked.

TWO EXTRA STEPS IN ACTION

While your competition:

- Tries to compete on price in saturated markets
- Attempts to be good at everything instead of great at one thing

- Follows standard industry practices
- Avoids doing difficult or uncomfortable things
- Focuses on their product instead of their customer experience
- Settles for average results

You will:

- Choose one area to dominate completely
- Do the research and extra work others won't do
- Create memorable, shareable experiences
- Build systematic processes for consistent delivery
- Charge premium prices for premium experiences
- Create a cult following and word-of-mouth marketing

That's how to create an unfair edge for yourself in a saturated market. Small differences in approach and execution create exponential differences in customer loyalty, pricing power, and business growth.

The market isn't too saturated for you to win. It's just waiting for someone willing to take the Two Extra Steps.

Chapter 5

CREATING DIFFERENTIATION

Is Taylor Swift the best singer in the world? No. Is she the best dancer? Not even close. But is she the most popular? Absolutely.

That's because Taylor Swift is super. She's figured out her superpower—and it's not her voice or her choreography. It's her ability to build a deep emotional connection with her audience. She is the absolute best in the world at making her fans feel seen, heard, and part of her world.

And I'll admit it: I'm a Swiftie. Everyone in my family is a Swiftie. We flew to Zurich, Switzerland, to see her perform after already seeing her live in Nashville. Why? Because she makes you feel like you're part of something bigger. That's the power of community connection—and it's her unfair advantage.

She leverages it everywhere: in her concerts, in her interviews, in the way she shows up on social media. She invites fans into her home. She throws private listening parties for them. She surprises people with handwritten notes, gifts, and inside moments. She's built an entire ecosystem where her audience isn't just buying albums or concert tickets—they're buying belonging.

Taylor isn't trying to be the best at everything. She's not competing on technical skill. She's dominating by doubling down on what she does best. That's why she sits at the very top while thousands of other technically gifted singers will never come close to her level of success.

This is exactly the principle you need to apply in your business. While most of your competition is out there trying to be decent at everything, you are going to identify your one thing—your superpower. The thing you can be absolutely world-class at. That's your separation. That's where 2 + 2 stops equaling 4 and starts equaling 5.

For you, that superpower might be personal connection like Taylor. It might be the way you build relationships with your customers. It might be your speed, your quality, your customer experience, or your ability to create something others simply can't replicate. The specific lever doesn't matter. What matters is that you intentionally pick something and build your entire business model around it.

Because when you do, you separate yourself from the pack. You create differentiation that your competition can't catch. And to help you find exactly where your superpower lives, I want to introduce you to one of the most important frameworks inside this book:

The Super Grader.

This is the simple, brutally honest tool I use to evaluate businesses across eight categories that separate winners from losers. Once you apply it to your business, you'll see clearly where your unfair advantage lives—and where your biggest opportunities to separate yourself truly exist.

THE SUPER GRADER FRAMEWORK: EIGHT CATEGORIES THAT SEPARATE WINNERS FROM LOSERS

And just as importantly, where you need to level up if you want to dominate.

Here's how it works . . .

First, you grade your business across all eight categories. When you're done, you'll have a total score—an honest snapshot of where you stand right now.

Then, you apply the exact same scoring system to your top competitors. Nine of them. No guesswork. No emotions. Just clear, side-by-side scores.

When you're done, the math tells the story. If you score a 77 and your competitors average 82, you know where you're losing ground. If you're sitting at an 84 and everyone else is struggling to break 70, you've already built real separation. This process gives you absolute clarity—both on where you stand today, and where you have the clearest opportunities to widen the gap.

Let's walk through the eight categories that make up your Super Grader.

CATEGORY 1: MEMORABILITY

First up: How memorable is your business? This is one of the most underestimated drivers of separation. Do people talk about you? Do they remember you? When your name comes up, does it stick?

Let me give you an example from my own life. I've used the same glass company for years here in Nashville. They've done shower doors for my house, glass installs for real estate projects, all kinds of jobs. But if you asked me right now to tell you the name of the company? I'd have to think about it. What I do remember is that their trucks are bright pink. That's it.

If I need to call them, I just type into Google: "glass company with pink vans Nashville." Immediately, Evans Glass pops up. I don't need to remember the name because the visual branding already did the job. Their pink vans made them memorable. And when people remember you, they can find you. That alone keeps your phone ringing.

You don't even have to be the best at what you do to win on memorability. You can have the second-best pizza in town, but if you're memorable while the number one guy isn't, you're still going to fill tables. If the fourth-best pizza shop has something unique that people remember—whether it's the packaging, the experience, or even just a ridiculous sign out front—they're still going to get attention.

I saw this again with my good friend Bobby Price. Bobby owned Price's Collision Center here in Nashville. He grew that business to 11 locations and more than $28 million a year before he sadly passed away. And a huge part of his success came down to one simple thing: jingles.

Bobby invested over a million dollars a year into radio ads. But it wasn't just the ad spend. It was the fact that he hired one of the best jingle writers in the country to create something that people couldn't forget. His commercials were everywhere, and the second you heard that jingle, it stuck in your head. Was Price's Collision necessarily better than every other body shop? Maybe. Maybe not. But when people got into a fender bender and had to make a split-second decision on where to go, they remembered Price's.

That's memorability. And it's one of the fastest ways to create distance between you and your competitors—simply by making sure people don't forget you when it matters most.

CATEGORY 2: STANDOUT FACTOR

What is it about your business that stands out? What makes you different from your competitors? This can take many forms. It might be price. It might be how you deliver your service. It might be speed.

Take McDonald's, for example. In my opinion, McDonald's might serve some of the worst fast food on the market. But when you need something fast, they are unmatched. They have mastered the art of speed. You pull off the freeway, hit the drive-through, and have food in your hand within minutes. That level of consistency in speed is their standout factor.

Now look at In-N-Out Burger. It operates on the opposite side of that equation. In-N-Out is not fast. The lines are long because demand is high. But they have built a brand around fresh food. They never freeze their ingredients, and the quality is far superior to typical fast food. If you are in a rush, you are probably not going to In-N-Out. You are going to McDonald's. But if you care more about food quality, you are willing to wait in line at In-N-Out.

The key question for your business is simple. What is your differentiator? What makes your business the obvious choice for your ideal customer? That is your standout factor.

CATEGORY 3: PRICING PSYCHOLOGY

Pricing plays a massive role in how your customers perceive the value of your product or service. The number you choose sets a psychological tone. It either creates perceived value or instantly eliminates it, depending on who you are trying to attract and what your competitors are charging. (More on this in the next chapter.)

If you are selling a luxury product, you want clean, round pricing. Luxury handbags do not cost $498.97. They cost $500. Premium services do not charge $19.88 a month. They charge $100 a month. That round pricing signals confidence and exclusivity.

On the other hand, if you are targeting discount buyers, the psychology flips. There is a reason Walmart uses pricing like $14.88 or $13.96. That pricing feels cheaper to a price-sensitive customer. Just being slightly below a round dollar creates the perception of a deal, even when the difference is pennies.

Your pricing sends a signal before anyone ever experiences your product. That signal tells your buyer which category you belong in and who your product is designed for.

CATEGORY 4: EASE OF DOING BUSINESS

How easy is it for your customer to do business with you? This is one of the most underrated factors that separates winning companies from losing ones.

When someone calls your business, do you pick up the phone within two rings? Or do you send them through an endless phone tree like a Fortune 100 bank, forcing them to press five different prompts just to speak with a human being? Every added layer creates friction. The more hoops your customer has to jump through, the more likely they are to give up.

If you are running an e-commerce business, how simple is it for someone to buy your product? Can they complete their purchase in a few clicks? Or do they have to create an account, confirm an email, enter redundant information, and stumble through multiple pages before they can check out?

The easier you make it to do business with you, the easier it becomes for your customers to give you their money. This is one of the biggest reasons Amazon scaled so quickly under Jeff Bezos. They eliminated friction. With one click, your order is placed. With Prime, it shows up in two days or less. They made it effortless.

The question for your business is whether you are making it effortless for your customer. If you are hard to reach, hard to buy from, or hard to navigate, you are giving your competitors an easy win.

CATEGORY 5: MARKETING EFFECTIVENESS

How effective is your marketing compared to your competitors? On a scale of one to ten, how strong are your messaging, your positioning, and your ability to generate interest that converts into sales?

Effective marketing does not just mean you have ads running. It means your message connects. It means your calls to action are clear and compelling. It means you are showing up where your customers spend their time and pulling them into your world.

Are your Facebook ads outperforming your competition? Are your Google search results ranking higher? Are you better at leveraging TikTok or Instagram Reels to reach your audience? Are your email open rates stronger than industry averages? Do people stop scrolling when they see your content?

Marketing effectiveness is not about shouting louder. It is about speaking directly to the customer you want and giving them a clear reason to engage. Strong marketing simplifies the buying decision. Weak marketing leaves customers confused, indifferent, or unaware you even exist.

CATEGORY 6: SALES PROCESS SPEED

How quickly can you close deals? This category has nothing to do with how many leads you generate. It is about how efficient you are once a qualified lead is in your pipeline.

Do you have a five-step sales process or a fifteen-step sales process? Have you refined and optimized that process to remove unnecessary friction? When a customer shows interest, how fast can you get them across the finish line?

Speed matters because buyer attention is fleeting. The longer your process drags out, the more time your competitors have to sneak in. The more complicated your steps, the more likely your prospect is to lose momentum or second-guess their decision.

You need to evaluate not just your close rate, but your close speed. How many touches does it take? How many meetings? How many days from first contact to signed deal? The faster you can move qualified prospects through your process without sacrificing quality, the more revenue you will capture.

CATEGORY 7: CLIENT RETENTION

This is where small businesses often fall apart. Retention is not just a nice-to-have. It is one of the most important drivers of long-term profitability.

Client retention measures what percentage of your customers continue doing business with you over time. When your sales team closes a deal, how many of those customers keep coming back? When someone buys your product online, do they return and make additional purchases? Are you building loyal customers, or is every sale a one-time transaction?

The higher your retention, the more stable your revenue becomes. You do not have to constantly acquire new customers to grow. You simply serve your existing ones better and keep them engaged. It costs far more to acquire a new customer than to keep an existing one, which is why retention is often the difference between profitable businesses and those that constantly feel like they are starting over.

Look at your own numbers honestly. Are you building relationships that keep people coming back? Are you offering reasons for your customers to stay loyal? If not, rate yourself accordingly on a scale of one to ten.

CATEGORY 8: LIFETIME VALUE

Lifetime value is where truly scalable businesses separate themselves from everyone else. This is not about what your customer spends on their first purchase. It is about what that customer is worth to you over the course of your relationship with them.

Do you have a sales ladder in place? Do you have a clear strategy that takes someone who spends $25 with you today and turns that into $100 over the next 12 months? Can you take that same customer and grow their value to $500 or more over the next two years?

This is what I call the ascension ladder. It is about guiding your customer through multiple offers, upgrades, cross-sells, and add-ons that naturally increase their total spend with you. You are not forcing them. You are building a business that serves their needs at higher and higher levels, with more valuable solutions at each step.

If you have no plan to grow the lifetime value of your customer, you are leaving money on the table. Worse, you are making it harder for your business to survive, because you are always chasing new customers instead of maximizing the ones you already have.

Be honest when you score yourself here. If you have no sales ladder or clear plan for increasing lifetime value, you are a one. If you have a fully mapped customer journey that ascends naturally over time, you are closer to a ten.

HOW TO IMPLEMENT THE SUPER GRADER

STEP 1: GRADE YOUR OWN BUSINESS

Start by evaluating your own business across all eight categories. Be brutally honest. The goal is not to inflate your score but to give yourself an accurate assessment of where you truly stand today. These customer-facing qualities are the foundation of your competitive advantage. When you calculate your total score, it will reveal exactly how strong your business is in its current state. If you score high, you are already positioned to build a Super company. If you score lower, you will clearly see where improvements are needed.

STEP 2: RESEARCH NINE COMPETITORS

Now it is time to look outside of your own business. Select nine competitors in your market and grade them using the exact same criteria you used for yourself. Be fair, objective, and consistent. This will take time because real research is required. Study their marketing. Analyze their pricing. Look at their customer experience, online reviews, and service models. Apply the same level of scrutiny you applied to yourself.

By the time you complete this step, you will have a dataset of ten businesses—your own plus nine competitors. You will see exactly where you rank within your market.

STEP 3: ANALYZE THE GAPS

The power of this exercise does not come from simply seeing a score. It comes from understanding why you assigned each score. Pay close attention to the reasoning behind every number you give. Take detailed notes on what your competitors do better than you and where they are falling short.

This is where you will start to uncover the specific gaps that exist in your market. If you are not yet at the top, this process will show you exactly what needs to be improved or added to your business to separate yourself from the competition. Every category you score lower in becomes an immediate action item and growth opportunity.

STEP 4: TAKE ACTION ON YOUR BIGGEST GAPS

Once you have your scores and your notes, you will have all the data you need to start building your Super business. The next step is simple: Act.

Start today. Do not wait for next week or next quarter. Identify the weaknesses holding your business back and begin fixing them now. Look at your competitors' offers and services. What are they providing that you are not? Which services or experiences are they charging for that you could begin offering in your own model?

Also look for opportunities to introduce vertical integration, just like Sam did in his business. By expanding your service offerings and controlling more of the customer experience, you not only create new revenue streams but also strengthen your customer relationships and build a business with greater stability and staying power.

STACKING MULTIPLE DIFFERENTIATORS TO CREATE A CATEGORY OF ONE

One of the biggest growth accelerators of my career came from a launch that hit harder than we ever expected. It was a SaaS company I cofounded with Scott Hill called MarketMySTR.com.

At the time, there was really only one competitor in the space. That competitor had similar software, sure, but it was priced like it was built for Fortune 500 companies. The cheapest plan started at $1,500 a month. For short-term rental hosts trying to grow, that price was a nonstarter. And that opened the door for us.

This was one of the rare times where I went in with the goal of competing on price, but with a huge catch: We weren't just going to be cheaper; we were going to overdeliver so aggressively on value that the price became a no-brainer.

We launched with three pricing tiers. Even our most expensive plan was still four times cheaper than their starting price. But that wasn't the real differentiator.

Before launch, we ran focus groups and listened. And what we heard was simple: The software wasn't the real problem. The real problem was that no one knew what to do with it. They didn't know how to write email sequences. They didn't know how to build landing pages or create content for their CRM. The tool didn't help if they had no idea how to use it.

That was the gap. And that's where we applied the Two Extra Steps.

We didn't just sell software. We delivered software that was already preloaded with:

- Done-for-you landing pages
- Website templates
- Swipe email sequences
- Social media templates
- 60-day launch road maps
- Built-in marketing automations

Instead of forcing people to start from scratch, we built it for them. All they had to do was customize it and go.

That one move separated MarketMySTR from every other SaaS company in the space. The competitor? Priced out of reach, overloaded with complexity, and leaving customers to figure it out all alone. We did the opposite. We made it simple.

And it worked. Within 60 days of launch, we signed up 538 customers—without a single paid ad, without outbound sales calls, without sales reps, and with 100% organic growth driven purely through influence and word of mouth. Our landing page converted at 28%. We were bringing in dozens of new customers daily with no formal sales process.

Why? Because the offer was complete. We solved every objection inside the offer itself. People didn't need convincing. They sold themselves. That's what happens when you stack so much value into your product that saying no feels stupid.

And we didn't stop there. Scott pushed the separation even further. He added 24/7 customer support—something almost nobody in our industry was doing. The competitor? You submitted a ticket and waited two or three days.

We gave our customers:

- Live chat 24/7
- Daily live Zoom coaching calls (Monday to Friday for the first 90 days)
- Real-time help with setup, automations, email copy, and landing page builds

We didn't just sell software. We built them an entire business inside the platform.

And the other thing we absolutely nailed was the copy. It was simple, visual, and easy to understand. No industry jargon. No fancy SaaS-speak. Just: "Here's what you get. Here's what it does. Here's how fast you can be up and running."

A lot of founders try to impress their prospects with complicated language, thinking complexity creates authority. It does the opposite. Complexity confuses. Simplicity sells.

We built the entire onboarding experience to be so simple that even someone who was completely overwhelmed with tech could be fully up and running in 60 days. That's why it worked.

THE SAM TRANSFORMATION STORY: FROM UBER DRIVER TO $4 MILLION LUXURY BUSINESS

Let me tell you about how the Two Extra Steps transformed a struggling transportation business into a luxury empire.

Eleven years ago, I was speaking at a conference in Las Vegas and a gentleman named Sam came up and introduced himself to me. He was dressed in jeans and an untucked polo shirt.

This was at a limousine and ground transportation conference. I was the keynote there, and he asked for my advice, so we sat down for a few minutes and he started telling me about his business.

THE PROBLEM: MISALIGNED WITH THE MARKET

He was basically an Uber driver who was now trying to service super high-end clients out of Park City and Deer Valley in Utah.

He told me about how he was trying to brand—he had his chauffeurs wearing jeans and vests and some of them were in cowboy boots because that's the "outdoorsy country theme" of being in Utah.

But he was operating as Uber and he was doing pickups, he was doing drop-offs, and he was trying to service super high-end hotels like the Montage and the Stein Eriksen. He was trying to service super high-end clients like Tony Hsieh, the founder of Zappos.

But he wasn't aligned with the buyers, so he didn't understand his buyer persona, and he built his company coming as an Uber driver into the luxury ground transportation space, but he was trying to deliver the low-end fast product that Uber delivered to clientele that had completely different expectations.

THE SOLUTION: COMPLETE BUSINESS TRANSFORMATION

I sat down with him for 30 minutes and started to deliver value for him, and we identified the buyer persona. We identified the extra steps that he needed to take to separate himself from where he was today, just to become competitive with the other limousine operators in the Park City and Salt Lake City markets.

Then we had to take the extra two steps to separate him from the competitors. So he had to take like four extra steps just to get to the level to even be competitive with the existing luxury ground transportation companies. Then he had to take the next Two Extra Steps to separate himself.

THE IMPLEMENTATION PROCESS

He became a one-on-one coaching client. We did calls every week. It's been 11 years that I've been coaching Sam, and it took him about a year to a year and a half to completely transition and go in and dominate that market.

His company, Four Seasons Concierge and Limousine Service in Park City and Salt Lake City, underwent a complete transformation. He rebuilt the brand from the ground up: the operations, the service delivery, the communication standards, the technology stack, the visual identity. Every touchpoint was elevated to move the business from an Uber-level experience to one that matched—and in many cases exceeded—the expectations of top-tier ground transportation companies.

The biggest shift happened on the front line with the chauffeurs. They went from wearing jeans and western shirts and vests and looking like cowboys to being black-suited, black tie, exuding the luxury dress code and training processes.

They were trained on interpersonal skills. They were trained on how to communicate or not to communicate with that high-end corporate traveler or that Russian oligarch that's coming to stay at Deer Valley, spending $20,000 to $30,000 a night on a short-term rental or staying at the Montage or the Stein Eriksen.

THE CONCIERGE GAME CHANGER

Most importantly, we changed his entire mindset of how to approach his business, being focused on that buyer persona, that ideal buyer that he wanted to try to acquire.

He went from a lower-end client that was looking for a cheap, fast ride to somebody that was willing to pay premium pricing for premium service.

He started offering concierge services, and he did this for Tony, the founder of Zappos, for about six months, right in the heart of COVID in 2020 and 2021. And honestly, when most ground transportation companies were failing, because Sam had implemented this type of concierge service at Four Seasons Concierge and Limousine Service, it's what kept him alive during COVID.

THE EXTREME SERVICE EXAMPLES

And he was doing crazy things that weren't even Two Extra Steps. They were three and four extra steps.

Sam told me one story when Tony had requested that he needed 120 iPads within 24 hours. That may seem ridiculous and I get that it is, but try to go buy just 10 or 20 iPads at one time. You can't do it online. You can't do it in one store. He literally pulled it off, and I have no idea how he did that.

Another story with Tony is that he had to procure 12 tour coach buses in less than a week. Tony wanted to have his own Burning Man out in the mountains of Wyoming close to Park City.

Those are the things that most people can't do. Those are the things that most people are unwilling to do because it takes so much time, so much effort. You don't have to have any expertise. You just have to know who to call, and you have to put in the effort.

THE RESTAURANT CONNECTIONS

That led to him creating Four Seasons Concierge, a total concierge service that would literally service the highest-end clients staying in Park City, staying in Deer Valley, for vacation.

He was so good at it that he ended up going out on his own. And now he has his ground transportation company and he has his concierge service.

The thing that separates Sam is that he can get his clients into any restaurant in Park City on a same-day notice when they're filled up and sold out. It could be Riverhorse on Main, or one of the good Italian places, or into the Stein Eriksen.

I remember calling him from the slopes in Deer Valley when I was skiing there with Eric Corson from my mastermind and Chris Wharton, my COO, and I said, "Hey, Sam, you told us that Stein Eriksen was a great place for brunch. Do you think you can get us in for lunch today and make us a reservation?"

This is literally at 11 o'clock in the morning. We wanted to get there at about noon. I had already called and they said they didn't have any capacity, so I put him on the spot.

But of course, with the magic of Sam and his relationships that he's built and what he's done for the Stein Eriksen, he was able to get us in and have lunch at 11:45—even faster than we had requested.

THE PROFITABILITY SHIFT

One of Sam's biggest moves was when we identified that $660,000 a year in revenue was a loss leader for him that he could not afford. He was actually losing about 8% on that revenue.

I'll never forget: We were at a mastermind meeting in Dallas, Texas, and we had to have an emergency triage with him. And then about two months later, he fired Delta.

What that did was free up space from an operational and a service delivery standpoint and from a mind space and personal time standpoint for him to focus on the things that would actually be profitable.

Sam was focused on revenue. I had him make a mindset shift to where he started being focused on profit.

He was more worried about keeping his vehicles on the road and his chauffeurs, his employees, busy and working than he was about his own profitability within the company. When that changed, it just started accelerating his growth.

THE RESULTS

Today he's around a $4 million a year business, has been since COVID, and his life has completely changed.

He's married to an incredible wife. He has an incredible business. He has automated sales processes and automation and dynamic pricing into his business to where he has eliminated about 75 to 80% of his workload in the ground transportation space so he can focus on growing his concierge business.

THE COMPLETE SUPER GRADER ASSESSMENT

Rate Each Category 1–10:

1. Memorability
   - Do people remember your brand?
   - Can they easily recall your business?
   - What makes you stick in their mind?
2. Standout Factor
   - What differentiates you from competitors?
   - Speed? Quality? Service? Price?
   - What's your unique positioning?
3. Pricing Psychology
   - Is your pricing aligned with your target market?
   - Does it create or destroy perceived value?
   - Luxury (round numbers) vs. discount (below round numbers)?
4. Ease of Doing Business
   - How simple is it to buy from you?
   - Phone answered quickly?
   - Smooth purchasing process?
5. Marketing Effectiveness
   - How strong is your messaging?
   - Quality of your advertising?
   - Online presence and conversion?
6. Sales Process Speed
   - How quickly do you close deals?
   - How many steps in your process?
   - What's your closing percentage?
7. Client Retention
   - What percentage of customers return?
   - How long do customers stay?
   - Repeat purchase rate?

8. Lifetime Value
    - Can you grow customer value over time?
    - Do you have an ascension ladder?
    - $25 customer → $100 → $500 progression?

Implementation Process

1. Grade yourself honestly across all eight categories.
2. Research and grade nine competitors using identical criteria.
3. Compare scores and identify your biggest gaps.
4. Take detailed notes on why competitors scored higher.
5. Create an action plan to address weaknesses.
6. Focus on becoming #1 in your biggest strength area.

THE SUPER GRADER ADVANTAGE

While your competition:

- Assumes they know how they stack up
- Focuses on what they think matters instead of what the customer values
- Tries to be good at everything instead of great at one thing
- Chases revenue over profitability
- Operates on gut feel rather than data
- Rarely commits to systematic improvement

You will:

- Systematically assess your business against your market
- Identify your unique superpower and double down on it
- Take honest inventory of weaknesses and aggressively fix them
- Prioritize profitability and fire unprofitable clients if needed
- Use data to guide business improvement
- Build a Super business that dominates the categories your ideal buyers care most about

Small differences in discipline, assessment, and focused execution create exponential differences in market position, pricing power, and long-term business results.

Most of your competitors will never do this work. They avoid it because it is uncomfortable, tedious, and forces them to confront reality. But that's why it works.

When you combine the Two Extra Steps with the insights from your Super Grader, you are no longer building your business by chance. You are building it with precision. And that is exactly how you create a Super business.

Chapter 6

PREMIUM PRICING

Pricing is one of the most misunderstood levers in business. And it is almost always where entrepreneurs leave the most money on the table.

Over and over in my career, I've raised my prices or launched products at pricing that was far above what my competitors were charging. Not because my product was radically different, but because I understood something most business owners never fully grasp: Pricing isn't simply math. Pricing is psychology.

Most entrepreneurs make the same mistake. They pick a price based on what feels reasonable. Or worse, they base it on what everyone else in their market is charging. Then they lock it in and never touch it again. The price becomes fixed in their mind, and they never test how far they could actually stretch it before hitting real resistance.

That's a massive mistake.

Because here's the truth: Very few pricing ceilings are as low as you think. In nearly every market, there's far more room to charge premium pricing than most people ever attempt. And when you get your pricing right, you unlock an entirely different business model. You don't have to grind for endless volume. You don't have to outwork your competitors to serve thousands of customers. You can build extreme profitability on fewer transactions, with better margins, better customers, and far less operational stress.

Look at luxury brands. Do you really believe a Louis Vuitton handbag costs 20 times more to produce than a Michael Kors bag? Of course not. The materials aren't radically different. The manufacturing isn't 20 times more expensive. What you're paying for is perception. Brand. Positioning. Status. Scarcity. Exclusivity. And that premium positioning allows Louis Vuitton to operate with margin profiles that their competitors can only dream of.

And here's the key: You don't have to be Louis Vuitton to apply this. The same pricing principles apply in every industry, at every level, if you understand how to use them.

While your competition races to the bottom, trying to win on discounts and undercut everyone else, you are going to take a completely different path. You are going to master pricing psychology and pricing elasticity. You are going to build a business where you need fewer customers to generate more profit.

MY FIRST LESSON IN PRICING

I learned my first real pricing lesson in high school, and it had nothing to do with business plans or spreadsheets. It started with a few T-shirts and an opportunity I never saw coming.

I met Jay Jacoby from American Pacific T-Shirts through junior golf in Southern California. After we played a round together, he handed me five T-shirts as a gift. They weren't Lakers shirts, which is what I would've picked. They were mostly big NBA names at the time: Scottie Pippen, Karl Malone, Charles Barkley, and, of course, Michael Jordan. I took them home, not thinking much of it.

When I got back to school, some of my friends on the basketball team saw the shirts and immediately wanted them. They were rare. You couldn't just walk into a store and buy them. Without really planning to, I sold those shirts to my friends for $30 each. At 16 years old, that felt like a fortune.

But when my mom found out, she was not thrilled. She told me I shouldn't have sold something that was given to me as a gift, and that I needed to tell Mr. Jacoby what I had done. A few months later, when we saw him again at another junior golf tournament, she marched me right up to him.

I admitted what I had done, expecting him to be upset. But instead, he surprised me. He smiled and said, "Good for you. You found demand." Then he said something that changed everything: "Why don't you and your mom come by my house after the tournament? I've got more shirts for you."

When we arrived, he handed me two full boxes of shirts. Easily 100 or 200 shirts, all new designs. "Take these back home and sell them at $30 apiece. I sell them wholesale for $12 to $15. You're already getting more than double what I get."

That was my first real exposure to pricing elasticity. I realized then that price wasn't determined by cost—it was determined by positioning and perceived value.

Back at home, I recruited two of my friends, Mike and Kevin. The three of us became partners in our first little business. We started hitting local high school football games, basketball games, tournaments—anywhere there were crowds of kids. And we weren't just selling to anyone. We positioned the shirts for athletes like us. These were rare designs that nobody else in Bakersfield could get their hands on. That scarcity created demand.

We even pushed the price higher. At a Christmas basketball tournament, we set up a table outside the gym and raised the price to $35 a shirt. And they still sold. In fact, they sold better than before. That taught me something I've carried forward into every business I've ever built: You don't know what the true price is until you test it.

Most business owners never test their pricing. They pick a number that feels "safe" or that matches what everyone else is charging, and they stop there. But when you really understand your customer, your positioning, and your product, you can stretch that pricing further than you think.

That simple T-shirt hustle became my first real-world pricing lab. And I've applied that exact principle ever since. Whether I was charging $19 per pound for brisket at Wild Bill's Texas Smokehouse when the local average was $9 or $10, or charging $125 for an airport transfer when everyone else in Nashville was charging $72, or launching our VIP concierge membership at $1,200 per month and selling out 100 memberships in 90 days—it all traces back to what I learned from selling those shirts.

If you truly understand the value you're providing and who you're selling to, you can charge premium prices. But you have to test, and you have to be willing to push the ceiling. That's how you uncover pricing elasticity. And that's how you start building profit models your competition never even attempts.

THE GRAND SELECT: HOW TO CREATE $1,200/MONTH PRICING

Now let me show you how this exact pricing principle played out on a much bigger scale later in my career. These weren't a few T-shirts. This was a seven-figure business model built on premium pricing, exclusivity, and one of the most powerful levers in business: access.

By now, you already know about Silver Oak, the ground transportation company I owned in Nashville. But here's what most people get wrong: We weren't in the limousine and chauffeur service—we were in the corporate travel and VIP service business.

Our core clients weren't bachelorette parties or prom kids. They were business executives, celebrities, athletes, and high-net-worth individuals who expected a level of service that most companies never even thought about delivering. That distinction mattered, because it shaped everything we did—from how we trained our chauffeurs to the way we handled every single client interaction.

Most of our competitors charged about $100 for a standard airport transfer in a sedan, or $125 for an SUV. It was a solid business, and we were already generating $5 million in annual revenue at that point. But I wanted to double it. I wanted to take us from $5 million to $10 million as fast as possible.

That's where Grand Select was born.

I realized something important about our client base: They had plenty of money. They could afford any car, any driver, any trip. What they didn't have was access. These people weren't price sensitive, but they were time sensitive. They valued convenience, status, and insider perks that most of our competitors couldn't offer.

So, instead of just trying to get more airport runs, I designed an entirely separate membership program that offered something they couldn't get anywhere else.

For $1,200 a month, our Grand Select members received:

- Two automatic vehicle upgrades per month. If they booked a sedan, we upgraded them to an SUV. If they booked an SUV, they could get upgraded to a Sprinter or Mercedes.
- A private VIP phone number. No phone trees. No waiting. Their calls went directly to a senior team member who handled their reservations personally.
- Guaranteed availability. Even during peak times, they had priority access to vehicles and drivers.
- Exclusive access to private clubs and events through our network of relationships in Nashville.

At the time, we were handling transportation for several high-profile clients: NFL players from the Tennessee Titans, country music stars like Tim McGraw and Faith Hill, Rascal Flatts, Keith Urban, and more. Many of them already used our service, but this program created a different level of relationship.

One of the biggest selling points was our ability to give them VIP access to the hottest private clubs in Nashville. At the time, there was a private venue called The Spot owned by John Rich and a few other investors. Membership at The Spot cost $17,500 a year, and even if you had the money, you still had to be invited in. Through Grand Select, our members could bypass the waitlist and get access immediately.

It was never really about the car service. It was about creating a feeling of exclusivity, access, and elevated status that nobody else in town was offering.

The results were almost immediate.

We capped the Grand Select program at 100 memberships to create scarcity and urgency. We sold out in less than 90 days. That was over a million dollars in new, recurring revenue—on top of our existing transportation business.

Even looking back today, I still shake my head at how simple it was. We weren't doing anything wildly complicated. The cars didn't change. The rides didn't change. But by understanding the value of access and packaging it properly, we created something completely different from the competition.

The opportunity was there the whole time. My competitors could have done the same thing. But they didn't. Because most businesses think they're selling a product or service. What they're really selling is the outcome their ideal buyer cares about most.

For our Grand Select members, it wasn't about transportation. It was about eliminating hassle, elevating status, and accessing perks that made their lives easier and more enjoyable. And because we designed the offer specifically for that buyer, they didn't flinch at the $1,200 price tag.

If you understand your customer deeply enough, you can create offers like this in almost any business. That's where pricing power comes from. Not features. Not hours. Not inputs. But outcomes.

When you sell outcomes instead of inputs, everything changes. You can charge more. You can serve fewer clients. Earn more profit with less volume.

But I didn't always get this right.

HOW I LEFT MILLIONS ON THE TABLE BY UNDERPRICING

I got into coaching when I was 24 years old, right after leaving a five-year run as a professional golfer. I'd chased the PGA Tour dream hard. Golf was my life. But when I met my wife, I realized building a future with her mattered more than grinding it out on the mini-tours.

So, I hung up the clubs and became the head golf coach at Cal State Bakersfield. It was only the second year of the program. They were a Division II school with powerhouse athletic programs in wrestling, basketball, and soccer. And there I was—a 24-year-old college dropout with no degree, no coaching experience, and a team of players barely younger than me.

I'll be honest . . . I felt like an impostor. Even though I'd been ranked third in the world as a junior and was one of the best players ever to come out of my town, I questioned everything I did. I second-guessed my decisions. I knew I needed help.

That feeling—the lack of confidence, the creeping doubt—followed me years later when I started my first business, and again when I stepped into coaching and consulting in 2012. By that point, I'd already built and scaled multiple companies. I'd exited businesses. I'd grown a limousine company into a multimillion-dollar operation. But when I launched my first coaching program, all the old doubts came rushing back.

And that's where the underpricing trap grabbed me. I let fear dictate my pricing. I looked at what everyone else was charging and told myself, *That's where I need to be.* I didn't fully understand that pricing isn't about what you think you're worth—it's about the outcomes you create and the confidence you have to own them.

THE SHIFT THAT CHANGED EVERYTHING

The real shift for me came from one of my early mentors, Jeff Walker. If you know anything about online business and digital coaching, you know

Jeff as the creator of Product Launch Formula, one of the most successful and widely used digital launch systems of all time.

Back when I first entered coaching, I purchased Jeff's program for $2,500. That was a huge investment for me at the time and it ended up changing everything for me. Not just because of the marketing strategy, but because of something Jeff taught about pricing itself . . .

"Whatever you think you should be charging, you're probably underpricing by at least 25 to 30 percent."

He explained that most of us chronically undervalue what we bring to the table because we see our own knowledge and expertise as "normal." We forget that what feels basic or obvious to us is completely transformative to the person who hasn't mastered it yet.

That advice was a gut punch for me because I knew he was right. I had been undervaluing my expertise for years.

Since that moment, I've adjusted my pricing strategy in coaching dramatically. I've now done over $60 million in coaching and program sales, across tens of thousands of students, and the results have been transformational for them and for me.

Charging more doesn't just create more income. It creates more impact.

Higher pricing allows me to reach more people, create higher-value experiences, and build programs that deliver better results. It allows me to invest heavily into free events, workshops, and resources that serve tens of thousands of people who may never pay me a dime, but still receive real value.

For example, my first live event—BNB Camp in Whitefish, Montana—cost me over $77,000 to host. Without premium pricing, that experience would never have been possible. Premium pricing on the front end funds the mission on the back end.

Premium pricing isn't just about profit. It's about building a business model that funds the bigger vision. Maybe that means giving back to your community, growing a world-class team, or, in my case, reaching one of my ultimate life goals: tithing a million dollars in a single year to my church.

That's why I work the way I do. That's why I charge premium rates. Because premium pricing doesn't just serve the business—it serves the mission.

If you're undercharging right now, you're not just leaving money on the table. You're limiting your impact. You're capping your ability to reinvest, hire, scale, and serve your clients at the highest level.

But let me be clear: This didn't come easy for me. For years, I fought the same battle you might be fighting right now. The math made sense, but the mindset didn't. I could build the systems. I could craft the offers. But when it came time to say the number out loud? Everything inside me resisted.

And the breakthrough didn't come from a business book. It came from one of the greatest sports psychologists in the world—and a lesson I first learned chasing the PGA Tour.

THE CONFIDENCE TO CHARGE MORE

When I was training to compete at the highest level in golf, I worked with Dr. Bob Rotella—the mental game coach behind countless major championships. Rotella has trained Ryder Cup stars and PGA legends, and his book *Golf Is Not a Game of Perfect* has become the ultimate playbook for mental toughness in sports.

If Michael Jordan had Phil Jackson for his mindset, golfers had Dr. Bob Rotella. He's the guy PGA pros trusted to sharpen their inner game when the difference between winning and losing came down to a single swing.

And here's what he drilled into me, over and over again:

"Perfect practice equals performance. You don't rise to the occasion—you rise to the level of your preparation."

That principle doesn't just apply to golf—it applies to business. And pricing is the same game.

If you want to command premium prices, you can't just "wing it" with what feels reasonable. You have to prepare. That's what most entrepreneurs miss. They think pricing power comes from clever marketing tactics or flashy branding. It doesn't. It comes from clarity, preparation, and practice—the same principles that win championships in sports.

Confidence is what lets you state your price without flinching, second-guessing, or negotiating against yourself. And confidence doesn't happen at the point of sale. It's built in the work you do long before—in what you do to understand your buyer and design an offer that truly solves their pain.

So, let's break down the framework I've used to build pricing power in every business I've ever run.

STEP 1: UNDERSTAND PRICE ELASTICITY

Price elasticity is simply the degree to which demand for your product or service changes when you adjust your pricing. In plain language: How much can you raise your price before it starts affecting sales volume?

Most entrepreneurs never explore this. They pick a price based on what their competitors are charging or what feels "reasonable," and then they get stuck there. But the smartest businesses constantly test how far they can stretch their pricing before hitting any real resistance.

You may find that you can increase your prices 20, 30, even 50% or more before sales start to slow. And often, once you establish a new price point, that higher price becomes the accepted norm for your brand.

Pricing isn't static. It's dynamic. It should evolve as your product improves, your reputation grows, and your ability to communicate value gets sharper.

STEP 2: TEST WITH YOUR TOP 10% OF CUSTOMERS

Your best insights almost always come from your best customers. These are the people who have already bought from you, who value what you do, and who are least sensitive to price increases if you continue to serve them well.

If you want to test price elasticity, start by having honest conversations with this group. Ask:

- What is the biggest pain point our business helps you solve?
- What would your world look like if we didn't exist?
- If we were able to provide even better results or service, what would that be worth to you?

When you understand the real outcomes your best customers are experiencing, you'll often realize that your pricing is wildly disconnected from the value you're delivering.

For example, let's say you're a plumber charging $175 per hour. Most plumbers max out around $185 to $195, maybe touching $200 if they're aggressive. But if you're consistently eliminating costly emergencies, saving your clients thousands in future repairs, and giving them peace of mind that no one else can offer, is that worth $250 or even $300 per hour to them? Many of your best clients will say yes.

The only way to find out is to ask.

STEP 3: RECOGNIZE THAT MOST BUSINESSES DON'T HAVE A PRICING PROBLEM

Here's one of the biggest pricing myths in small business: "My prices are too high; that's why people aren't buying."

In reality, most businesses don't have a pricing problem. They have a customer acquisition problem.

They are attracting the wrong buyers. They are marketing to the price-sensitive crowd who shops based on cost alone, rather than targeting buyers who value results, quality, convenience, or access. This is why having a clearly defined buyer persona matters so much. If you're constantly hearing price objections, you don't need cheaper prices. You need better-qualified buyers.

STEP 4: BUILD VALUE PROPOSITIONS THAT SUPPORT PREMIUM PRICING

If you want to command premium prices, you need to support them with premium value. That doesn't mean more features. It means more outcome. More convenience. More access. More peace of mind.

Let's say you're selling beach towels. The fact that your towels dry faster, are softer, and hold up longer than anything else on the market—that's your value proposition. You build the story around that. You position it as the solution to your customer's problem, not just another towel.

Premium pricing isn't about the product alone. It's about how well you demonstrate the pain you're solving and the transformation you're delivering.

STEP 5: UNDERSTAND WHAT YOU'RE REALLY SELLING

This is where most business owners get it wrong. You are never selling the product. You are selling the outcome.

Louis Vuitton doesn't sell handbags. They sell status. Exclusivity. The feeling of being seen as someone important. That's why a Louis Vuitton bag can sell for $4,000 while another bag that carries the same items might sell for $150.

The product itself isn't 30 times better. But the perceived value, the identity attached to ownership, and the brand association all combine to justify premium pricing.

And that principle applies no matter what you sell.

Whether you are a service provider, a product-based business, or even a coach or consultant, you are never selling "what" you do. You are selling who your customer becomes after working with you.

THE PSYCHOLOGY OF LUXURY VS. DISCOUNT PRICING

THE PSYCHOLOGY OF LUXURY VS. DISCOUNT PRICING

Understanding pricing psychology means understanding how different types of buyers think. And at the most basic level, there are two completely different mindsets: discount buyers and luxury buyers. They do not think the same way. They do not shop the same way. And if you apply the wrong pricing psychology to the wrong customer, you lose margin, you lose volume, or you lose both.

DISCOUNT PRICING PSYCHOLOGY (THE WALMART MODEL)

Walmart is speaking to discount buyers. These are price-sensitive shoppers. They are trained to look for small savings. And if you've ever really looked at the prices, you'll notice something: They almost never use even, rounded numbers. You don't see $15 or $12 on the shelf. You see prices like $14.87, $29.73, $10.43.

Discount buyers respond to the idea that $14.87 feels cheaper than $15, even though the difference is minimal. The psychology is that you're getting a deal, and that triggers the emotional response they're looking for.

Even the rollback pricing works the same way. It rarely lands on a round dollar amount. It will roll back to something like $13.43 instead of $14. That is intentional. That is pricing psychology.

This kind of buyer isn't concerned with exclusivity, status, or premium experience. They're shopping on price, and they want to feel like they're getting maximum value for the lowest possible cost.

If your business is positioned for a discount buyer, this is the psychology you're dealing with. The closer you can edge your price just below the next whole number, the more attractive it feels to that customer. But you need to be very intentional about whether these are the customers you want to serve, because building a business around price-sensitive buyers requires massive volume to succeed.

LUXURY PRICING PSYCHOLOGY (THE LOUIS VUITTON MODEL)

Now let's flip to the complete opposite end of the spectrum. Look at companies like Louis Vuitton or Patek Philippe. These are extreme luxury brands, and their pricing reflects that.

You won't see a Louis Vuitton handbag priced at $3,987.53. It's $4,000. You won't see a Patek Philippe watch priced at $37,632.11. It's $40,000. Round, clean, even numbers.

Why? Because luxury buyers are not looking for deals. They are not thinking in terms of small savings. In fact, adding decimal points or odd pricing would actually cheapen the brand in their eyes.

Luxury buyers associate round numbers with status, exclusivity, and prestige. The pricing itself becomes part of the positioning. The clean, even price signals that this is not something you buy on sale. This is something you invest in because of what it represents.

Luxury pricing isn't just about charging more. It's about sending the right message to the right buyer. It creates confidence. It reinforces the story that the product is in a category of its own, not something to be compared on price with competitors.

WHY THIS MATTERS FOR PRICING ELASTICITY

When you start testing pricing elasticity in your business, you aren't just testing numbers. You are testing positioning. How you present your price is just as important as the amount itself.

If you're selling to luxury buyers, round numbers create confidence. If you're selling to discount buyers, psychological pricing just below whole numbers creates urgency and perceived savings.

This distinction is absolutely critical if you want to fully maximize your pricing power. Because pricing isn't just about what your product costs. It's about how your ideal customer emotionally responds to the price you're presenting.

THE MONTHLY RECURRING REVENUE STRATEGY

If you're a plumber, an HVAC company, or any type of service-based business, you should seriously consider adding monthly recurring revenue (MRR) to your model. It is one of the most powerful ways to stabilize cash flow, increase the value of your business, and smooth out the roller coaster of unpredictable revenue.

MRR is the gold standard for both cash flow management and business valuation. Businesses with strong recurring revenue models are more predictable, more stable, and far more valuable when it comes time to sell or raise capital.

Let's say you're a plumber currently charging $175 an hour for service calls. You might feel pressure to raise your rate to $225 or $275 to improve margins. But instead of chasing higher hourly rates, you could approach it differently. You could actually lower your hourly rate to $155, positioning yourself below market price while adding a recurring membership on top of it.

For example, you create a membership plan where customers pay $99 per month. That membership includes priority scheduling, same-day or 24-hour service, waived after-hours fees, and discounts on parts or repairs. In return, you're locking in predictable monthly revenue whether your customer needs a service call that month or not.

Now look at the math. The average homeowner may only need plumbing services once a year, for a couple hours at most. Under your old model, they'd pay $175 an hour, maybe $350 total for a two-hour job. But with the new structure, your hourly rate is $155 (saving them $20 per hour), while they're also paying $99 a month on retainer. That's nearly $1,200 a year in recurring revenue, regardless of how often they actually need service.

You've made your pricing more attractive up front, while locking in far more revenue on the back end. And just as importantly, you're creating a relationship with your customer that extends year-round, not just when something breaks. That's where real business value lives.

This is how you create leverage with pricing models that reward you for consistency rather than one-off transactions. Monthly recurring revenue isn't just about charging more. It's about stabilizing your business and creating reliable, predictable growth.

THE TESLA ADVANTAGE: PRICING POWER IN ACTION

Every major automaker now sells an electric vehicle. Ford has the F-150 Lightning. Porsche has the Taycan. BMW and Mercedes have their luxury EVs. On paper, some of these cars match or beat Tesla in features. So why does Tesla still lead in pricing power and why do customers pay it?

They redefined the buying experience and positioned the brand as premium.

Tesla made it easy to buy an EV without the traditional dealership grind. Transparent pricing. No haggling. Delivery to your driveway. That simplicity became part of their value and people pay for it.

They wrapped the product in scarcity.

Tesla uses waitlists and delivery timelines strategically to maintain demand tension. Even when competitors are discounting heavily, Tesla rarely cuts prices because that would erode its premium positioning.

They sell identity, not just a car.

Tesla buyers aren't just purchasing a vehicle. They're buying status, innovation, and a sense of belonging to the future. That identity justifies premium pricing because it turns the car into a statement.

Tesla's costs haven't risen in proportion to their price increases over the years. The gap between cost and price is where margin lives—and Tesla has mastered creating that gap. They've built a story so strong that people pay $60,000, $80,000, even $100,000 for something other companies sell for less.

That's pricing elasticity in action.

FEWER CUSTOMERS, MORE PROFIT

Here's what most small business owners fail to realize. When you have pricing power, you don't need as many customers. You don't need to produce as much product. The higher your pricing, the fewer buyers you need to generate the same or even greater revenue.

Let me say that again: Higher price point equals fewer customers. That means your customer acquisition doesn't necessarily become easier, but it becomes more focused and far more efficient. You can produce less product, serve fewer customers, and still increase profitability.

For example, let's say I'm running a restaurant that sells watermelon dishes. I sprinkle them with sea salt, add some toppings, and charge $10 per plate. But if I position the product as limited, exclusive, or part of a high-demand trend, I may be able to charge $15 for the exact same dish.

Now, imagine I only prepare 100 servings per day, and every day they sell out by noon. That 50% price increase means I generate significantly more revenue while producing the same amount of product.

At the same time, my labor and overhead costs may actually decrease because I'm not scrambling to increase volume. My profitability rises simply because I've created a premium product with built-in demand, scarcity, and pricing power.

This is exactly what I call a Super product.

THE PAIN-TO-SOLUTION FRAMEWORK

The Pain-to-Solution framework is powerful for understanding how to price, position, and sell any product or service. And it all comes down to one visual.

THE PAIN-TO-SOLUTION FRAMEWORK

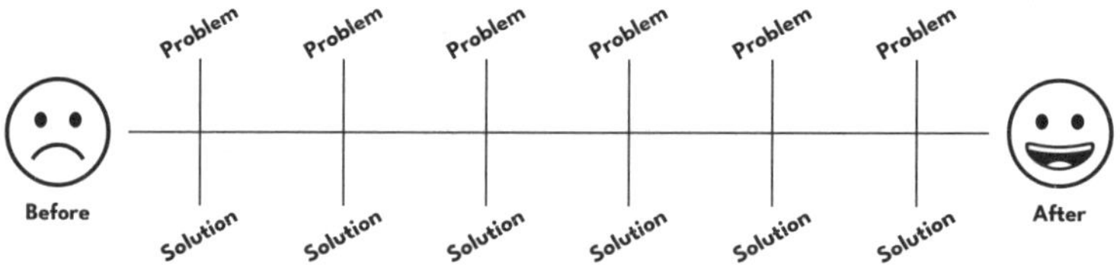

The sad face on the far left represents where your customer starts—the problem they're dealing with today. The frustration. The thing keeping them stuck. On the far right, you've got the happy face—this is where your customer wants to be. The problem is solved. The frustration is gone. The transformation is complete.

In between are the steps. Each slash represents a pain point the customer is feeling. For every pain point listed above the slash, your job is to map out the solution you provide directly beneath it.

For example:

- Pain: "I don't have enough time."
- Solution: "We do it for you."
- Pain: "I don't know who to trust."
- Solution: "We guarantee results and provide social proof."

Your entire product, your marketing, and ultimately your pricing are built around how many of these pain points you can eliminate. The more pain you solve, the more value you create and the more pricing power you have.

Because, at the end of the day, you're not selling features. You're selling outcomes. You're taking someone who is frustrated and giving them relief. You're turning the sad face into the happy face. That's the core of real pricing power.

It's exactly like calming a toddler. You've got a two-year-old on the floor, mid-meltdown. Screaming. Flailing. Completely inconsolable. You hand them something they love—a pacifier, a lollipop—and instantly, the crying stops. The meltdown turns to calm. The problem vanishes.

That's what your product or service has to do for your customer. You find the lollipop that solves their biggest frustrations. You remove pain. You deliver relief. That is what unlocks pricing elasticity and allows you to move into premium pricing territory.

When you deeply understand your customer's pain and match your solution to eliminate it, you can command higher prices, serve fewer customers, and create dramatically more profit.

SHORT-TERM RENTAL REALITY CHECK

As I'm writing this, a lot of short-term rental owners across the country are struggling. You see it in markets like the Smoky Mountains, Panama City Beach, Orlando, Branson, Destin, Gulf Shores—all the big, popular vacation rental areas.

But the reason most of these owners are struggling isn't what they think.

They're not failing because the market is saturated. They're failing because they bought average properties that look like everyone else's. They're not unique. They don't stand out. And because they're average, they get trapped in price competition.

Their real problem isn't market saturation. It's product mediocrity.

Most of these owners bought homes that check the generic boxes: decent location, clean interior, some basic amenities. But nothing memorable. Nothing differentiated. Nothing that creates a reason for someone to pick their property over the dozens of others nearby. And when that happens, they're left competing on price, trying to undercut the competition just to stay booked.

That's not a pricing problem. That's a positioning problem.

When you have a product that's truly Super—something uniquely designed for a specific buyer, with features and experiences nobody else is offering—you no longer have to compete on price. You create pricing power because your guests want what you have, not just any random short-term rental.

This same principle applies to every business, not just short-term rentals. If you find yourself constantly battling price objections, discounting to fill your pipeline, or losing deals to competitors, the problem usually isn't your price point—it's your product positioning.

Average businesses die in crowded markets. They get swallowed up by better operators who took the time to design something differentiated.

That's why you see companies like Kmart, Sears, Ruby Tuesday, and Gap disappear while other brands thrive. They were average. And average gets crushed.

Super businesses stand out, command premium pricing, and thrive—even in saturated markets.

You've seen how pricing elasticity works in the real world, but examples only get you so far. Now let's break down exactly how to apply these principles to your own business step by step, so you can systematically test, adjust, and build pricing power over time.

THE COMPLETE PRICING ELASTICITY SYSTEM

This is the step-by-step system you can apply to any business to maximize pricing power and profitability.

STEP 1: CREATE A FOCUS GROUP WITH THE TOP 10% OF CUSTOMERS

Start with your best customers. These are the ones who already value your product or service the most.

- Ask them directly: What is the biggest pain your business has solved for them?
- Ask what their biggest challenge was before finding your solution.
- Gauge how much more value they would place on your service if you solved even more of those pain points. Test how far you can stretch your pricing based on the value you've already delivered.

The answers will reveal where you have room to increase prices without damaging demand.

STEP 2: UNDERSTAND YOUR PRICING PSYCHOLOGY

Your pricing presentation matters as much as your pricing itself.

- Discount buyers respond to psychological pricing: odd numbers, decimals, and pricing just under round numbers. Think $14.87 or $29.73.
- Luxury buyers respond to simple, round pricing: $500, $1,000, $10,000. Round numbers signal confidence, exclusivity, and status.

The price format signals who your product is designed for.

STEP 3: CREATE UNIQUE VALUE PROPOSITIONS

If you want to justify premium pricing, you must solve bigger problems and eliminate more pain. This could look like:

- Adding convenience
- Eliminating friction
- Providing better outcomes
- Offering access others cannot

Price follows value. The more problems you solve, the higher your price can go.

STEP 4: TEST MULTIPLE PRICE POINTS

Do not pick one price and stick with it forever. Test. Measure. Repeat.

- Start by increasing prices 25 to 30%.
- Test different service tiers or bundles.

- Experiment with monthly recurring revenue models to stabilize cash flow.
- Introduce VIP or membership levels that deliver access or exclusivity.

STEP 5: POSITION SCARCITY AND EXCLUSIVITY

Scarcity drives urgency. Exclusivity creates desire.

- Limit availability.
- Cap membership programs.
- Offer unique access that others cannot replicate.

The perception of limited access raises perceived value and supports premium pricing.

STEP 6: FOCUS ON OUTCOMES, NOT FEATURES

You are not selling features. You are selling relief from pain and frustration.

- Show how your product transforms your customer's experience.
- Demonstrate how you turn their "sad face" into a "happy face" by removing obstacles or solving problems.
- The outcome is what earns pricing power.

THE TWO EXTRA STEPS PRICING ADVANTAGE

While your competition:

- Keeps pricing static and guesses what customers will pay
- Chases volume instead of maximizing value
- Competes on price rather than outcomes

- Attracts price-sensitive buyers who drain profit
- Fails to differentiate themselves

You will:

- Systematically test and stretch your pricing
- Create clear value propositions your competition cannot match
- Use psychological pricing that attracts your ideal buyer
- Build recurring revenue for stability and scale
- Deliver outcomes that justify premium pricing

That's how premium pricing becomes your Two Extra Steps advantage. Small differences in positioning, testing, and value creation lead to exponential differences in profitability with fewer customers.

Remember: You don't have a pricing problem—you have a customer acquisition problem. When you attract the right buyers with the right positioning, they'll pay premium prices for solutions that eliminate their pain and deliver the outcomes they desperately want.

Chapter 7

MARKETING AND SELLING YOUR PREMIUM PRODUCT

Most entrepreneurs market the wrong thing.

They obsess over the product itself. They market features, benefits, lists of what's included. They believe that if they just explain what the product does, people will naturally want to buy it. But that's not how premium marketing works.

If you want premium pricing, you can't just sell the product. You have to market the outcome. You have to market the feeling your buyer wants to experience after the product solves their problem.

Premium products are sold through positioning, not through lists of features. The brands that dominate don't compete by offering more features—they create demand by making the customer feel something no competitor can replicate.

That's where most businesses fall flat. They're selling information. You're going to sell transformation.

Because when you create unique value propositions, when you build exclusivity, when you speak directly to your buyer's pain points and desires, you unlock the ability to charge premium prices and attract buyers who aren't price sensitive. While your competition markets features and fights over price, you'll market outcomes and create demand.

That's your Two Extra Steps advantage.

Now let me show you exactly how this works—and how one of the biggest breakthroughs of my career happened completely by accident.

WHEN A MISTAKE CREATED A MULTIMILLION-DOLLAR USP

One of the best lessons I've ever learned about marketing a premium product came from a complete accident.

Back in 1992, while playing on the South American PGA Tour in São Paulo, Brazil, I stayed with a local family who made handmade Brazilian swimwear—wraps, sarongs, bikinis—all by hand, right there in their small home. At first, I didn't think much of it. But when I returned to Brazil the following year, something clicked.

I brought an extra suitcase and packed it full of bikinis, wraps, and sarongs. And when I got back home to Bakersfield, California, I launched Bell Aqua Bikinis.

Now keep in mind, this was 1992. There was no Shopify. No Facebook ads. I spent nearly every dollar I had earned that year building one of the very first e-commerce websites for a drop-shipping business at a whopping cost of $180,000. It took over six months to complete, all running on AOL chatrooms, Netscape browsers, and early email lists.

But here's where everything changed: We made a mistake.

I had my friend John helping with order fulfillment while I was playing a tournament. And John completely screwed up dozens of orders. He mismatched sizes, mixed patterns, sent out tops that didn't match bottoms, and shipped out combinations that had never been paired together.

At first, I was furious. But what we didn't realize at the time was that this mistake created something the swimwear industry had never seen before.

Up until that point, women's swimwear was sold as matching sets: small top with small bottom, medium with medium, large with large. You couldn't mix and match. You couldn't pair a floral bottom with a striped top. You couldn't get different sizes for each piece to fit your body. It was rigid.

But John's fulfillment mistakes accidentally introduced a completely new buying experience. Women who received these mismatched orders loved it. They suddenly had options. They could mix patterns. They could buy a medium bottom and a large top. They could finally customize the fit, the look, and the style.

It was a total accident that ended up becoming our unique value proposition.

That one differentiation created enough momentum that Bell Aqua was eventually acquired by the largest swimwear company in the industry at the time, Venus Swimwear. And it taught me one of the most important marketing lessons of my life:

Uniqueness creates leverage.

When you create something unique—whether intentionally or by accident—you open up marketing doors your competitors can't walk through. You no longer have to fight over price, features, or specifications. You market the uniqueness itself.

That's what separates premium products from average ones. Super from subpar.

CREATING 50%+ CONVERSION RATES

One of the most effective premium marketing campaigns I've ever built is one that's still running today: my Inner Circle mastermind.

The concept was simple, but the execution followed everything you're learning in this book: unique value, exclusivity, accessibility, and marketing to the exact right buyer.

THE UNIQUE OFFER: THE TWO EXTRA STEPS

Most coaching programs are broad. They cover too much, or they rely on generalists trying to teach everything. I built Inner Circle differently. I didn't hire generalists. I went out and found the best in each discipline.

- The best revenue manager
- The best property finder
- The best interior designer
- The best lender
- The best marketer
- The best software and tech expert
- The best attorney
- And several more across the full spectrum of real estate investing

Instead of one coach pretending to do it all, I assembled a team of elite specialists. My members don't get watered-down advice. They get the best insights available in each lane, directly from the people living it at the highest level.

But even more important than the experts was the accessibility.

THE 5 AM CLUB: AVAILABILITY AS DIFFERENTIATION

In the coaching world, accessibility is rare. Most gurus make you jump through hoops to get in touch. They hide behind layers of assistants or charge extra for personal access.

I did the opposite. I created what I call the 5 AM Club.

Monday through Friday, my normal workday is packed. So I offer members something almost nobody else does: personal access to me at 5 AM. If they're willing to get up early and take their Two Extra Steps, I'll meet them there and match that effort.

That level of availability became one of the most valuable, talked-about parts of the Inner Circle experience. It created an intimacy and a trust that most coaching programs simply don't offer—and my members knew it.

THE ULTRA-EXCLUSIVE LAUNCH: NO WEBSITE, NO ADS

When I launched the Inner Circle in December 2021, I didn't build a website. I didn't run Facebook ads. I didn't create a long sales page. Instead, I invited 20 people personally handpicked from my most active, engaged members inside my Facebook group. These were the people already showing up. They were engaged, asking questions, taking action.

Out of 20 personal invitations, 15 said yes. That's a 75% close rate with zero advertising spend.

After that initial group, I kept the offer intentionally hidden. The only way to join Inner Circle was to attend one of my live boot camps. No public links. No Google searches. You had to be invited or show up in person.

At one of our early boot camps, we had about 50 to 60 attendees. Before I even presented the offer, I brought five of my original Inner Circle members onstage for a live Q&A, letting them share their own experience.

Then I opened enrollment. By the end of the event, 31 people joined—more than a 50% conversion rate into a $10,000 program.

And those members? Most are still in the program today.

WHY IT WORKED: EXCLUSIVITY AND SCARCITY

This wasn't luck. It was deliberate.

- We made it hard to access.
- We built exclusivity into the process.
- We created real urgency by limiting enrollment windows.
- And we stacked unique value that no other coaching program in the space could match.

The combination of extreme value, hyper-targeted buyers, and controlled exclusivity is exactly why Inner Circle scaled the way it did, without needing mass marketing, complicated funnels, or constant sales pushes.

When you make your offer exclusive, you create desire. When you pair exclusivity with real value that cannot easily be copied, you create demand. And when you control both access and delivery, you can charge premium pricing while maintaining exceptionally high client satisfaction and retention.

HOW SOLVING PAIN BECOMES A MARKETING ADVANTAGE

Let me give you one of the clearest examples of how identifying and solving pain creates instant market differentiation.

Buying a car is one of the most universally painful consumer experiences there is. Everybody dreads it. You walk onto a lot and within 30 seconds someone's hovering. You get passed off from one salesperson to another. You sit through endless back-and-forth negotiations where the sales manager "needs to check with corporate." You finally agree on price, and then the real waiting game starts. You get funneled into finance, sit through the warranty pitch, wait again for paperwork processing, and easily burn three or four hours—or more—just to drive home with your car. It's exhausting. It's inefficient. And most importantly—it's avoidable.

I recently helped my mother-in-law buy a new Ford Explorer, and I saw a perfect opportunity to avoid all that pain. She already knew the exact vehicle she wanted. I found one at a dealership, and I called them directly as her son-in-law, making it crystal clear up front that we were ready to buy and paying in cash.

I negotiated everything over the phone before my wife and her mom even got in the car. But then I went one step further and solved the real problem. I told the dealership:

"I'm sending my wife to pick her up. It's about a 45-minute drive to her house, and another hour to get to you. I don't want them sitting there for half the day. Have the vehicle cleaned, detailed, gassed up, and parked out front. Have the paperwork completely ready to sign. The only thing I want them doing is reviewing and signing documents. Because if they sit around waiting for hours like most people do, they're going to leave."

The sales manager promised he would personally handle it. And to their credit, they delivered. My wife and mother-in-law were in and out in less than 45 minutes. From arrival to driving off the lot, they spent less time buying the car than they did driving to the dealership.

Now compare that to the traditional experience most people endure: endless haggling, multiple sales desks, long waits for finance managers, warranty upsells, contract processing delays, and a general sense of frustration that burns an entire afternoon. It's an awful process almost everyone expects and dreads.

That is exactly why this becomes such a powerful marketing advantage.

If you own a dealership, you don't need to promise the lowest prices to win. You don't need to race to the bottom like your competitors. You simply eliminate the pain your customers are already bracing for. You position your dealership as the easiest, fastest, most streamlined buying experience in your market. You turn the car-buying process into something that feels respectful, efficient, and even enjoyable.

And here's the most important part: People will literally choose to come to you just for the experience. Even if your cars aren't priced lower. Even if you don't carry every make and model. Even if they weren't considering your dealership initially.

Because once you solve a pain people hate that much, you separate. That's the entire point of Two Extra Steps. You're not just selling cars. You're selling relief. And when your marketing speaks to that pain directly, your competitors can't touch you.

THE AIRBNB FEELING EXAMPLE

Let's shift gears for a second, because this exact same principle applies to any business—whether you're selling cars, coaching programs, or vacation rentals like I do with my Airbnbs.

In short-term rentals, most people focus entirely on the booking process. They obsess over occupancy rates, nightly pricing, listing photos, and calendar optimization. All of those things matter, but they're not what creates a premium brand or true customer loyalty. The real leverage point is much simpler than most people realize: how the guest feels when they leave.

For me, the most important moment in my Airbnb business isn't when someone books. It's not when they check in. It's not even during their stay. The moment that matters most is when they walk out the front door, load the car, buckle their kids in, and hit the START button to head home.

Because right there, in that exact moment, one of two things happens:

- They either feel like they just had an amazing experience that was easy, comfortable, and worth every penny . . .
- Or they're sitting in that car feeling disappointed, frustrated, or let down . . . swearing they'll never book with you again.

There's almost no middle ground.

That's where your marketing is actually created. Not in the listing description, but in that final emotional impression they drive away with. If you get that right, you don't need discounts or gimmicks. You don't need to constantly hustle for your next booking. You've created word-of-mouth, repeat business, glowing reviews, and social proof that your competitors can't buy.

What creates that feeling? It's the Two Extra Steps. The tiny details that most hosts skip because they assume guests won't notice.

- The fully loaded kitchen with spices, pots, pans, utensils, plastic wrap, and every extra imaginable that makes life easier.
- The coffee bar in the master bedroom so the booker can have coffee without leaving the room.
- The extra phone chargers by the nightstand because someone always forgets theirs.

Why do these matter? Because they remove friction. They reduce mental load. They create ease. And when guests leave with that feeling, they associate your property with a premium experience.

One worth paying more for. One worth telling their friends about. One they actively seek out again on their next trip.

That's the Two Extra Steps principle in action.

You're not just providing a bed and a roof. You're creating an emotional outcome that stacks value far beyond your competitors who are still playing the commodity game.

When you solve emotional pain points that nobody else is addressing, you create built-in marketing. That feeling becomes your advertising. And when your customers feel the difference, they will pay for the difference.

THE CYCLICAL NATURE OF CUSTOMER SATISFACTION

Even when you nail the feeling, even when your customers leave happy, the reality is that satisfaction doesn't last forever. Human nature kicks in. People are always scanning for something better. That's where the real marketing work begins.

The truth is, there are only two reasons customers leave a brand.

- Either they're frustrated because something didn't meet their expectations.
- Or they believe there's a better option out there.

Both of those situations trigger the same thing: pain. The customer gets that sad face again. And now they're back on the hunt, looking for someone who can solve that pain better than the last company did. The minute they find a product, service, or experience that feels better, faster, easier, or more valuable—their face turns back to happy, and they switch.

This is why your marketing is never done. It's why your positioning has to constantly stay sharp. Every single pain point you've mapped out on your worksheet is not just a sales problem; it's a marketing opportunity. Each one is another reason your future customers are actively out there, right now, looking for you to fix what someone else didn't.

THE PREMIUM MARKETING FRAMEWORK

So let's break down exactly how to build marketing systems that capitalize on this cycle and turn that pain into premium positioning.

STEP 1: CREATE SOMETHING UNIQUE

First, you have to have something unique. If you don't, everything else we're about to cover becomes 10 times harder. Your uniqueness is what gives you permission to charge more, attract better customers, and dominate your market.

This is the first big fork in the road for most businesses. Most stay safe. They copy the herd. They build businesses that look and sound just like everyone else. And then they wonder why they're stuck fighting for scraps.

I learned this lesson the hard way early in my career: If you don't create uniqueness on purpose, you end up lost in the middle lane.

And that middle lane? That's where businesses go to die.

You're not fast enough to outrun your competition. You're not cheap enough to win the price war. You're not premium enough to command top dollar. You're just there—getting passed on both sides.

In every business I've built, I've made it my mission to avoid that middle lane at all costs. I want to either be in the slow lane by choice (for control), or in the fast lane flying at 85. And if you've followed me long enough, you know where I live. Full throttle, fast lane, all day.

STEP 2: USE THE PROBLEMS AND SOLUTIONS WORKSHEET

Every single problem and solution you identified on your worksheet is not just helpful data. It's your marketing gold mine. Each one gives you a clear opportunity to speak directly to the real pain your ideal customer feels every day.

Problems	Solutions

The more you lean into those problems, the more attention you'll capture. Because that's what marketing really is: problem agitation. You want your ideal customer to feel, in their gut, that you understand exactly what frustrates them and that you have the solution.

This is where most businesses stay too soft. They list features. They talk about benefits. But they don't dig deep enough into the pain. Your job is to turn up the volume.

If you mapped out three pain points? Push it to five. If you've got five? Stretch it to seven. The more angles you can pull out, the more emotional hooks you create. And the more you agitate those pain points, the more valuable your solution feels.

This is what earns you pricing power. This is how you move into super-premium positioning.

Because when you've exposed seven points of pain and your competitor only talks about three, your customer will always believe your solution is more complete, more valuable, and worth paying more for.

That's how you separate yourself. That's how you earn the right to charge premium prices, to sit above Louis Vuitton in your market. You are not just selling a product. You are solving more pain, more completely, than anyone else.

STEP 3: MASTER YOUR IDEAL BUYER

When you know exactly who your ideal buyer is, your marketing stops being complicated. You're no longer guessing, hoping, or throwing out generic ads. You're speaking directly to the person who is already most likely to say yes.

The more deeply you know your buyer, the easier everything becomes. What do they care about? What keeps them up at night? What magazines do they read? What shows do they binge? What car do they drive, what hobbies do they have, what neighborhoods do they live in? These aren't just interesting facts. They are your targeting blueprint.

For example, if you're running Facebook ads, the entire platform runs on interests, behaviors, and demographics. The more accurate your buyer profile, the better Facebook (or any other platform) can put your message in front of the exact people who want what you sell.

And it goes far beyond audience selection. Your copy changes depending on who you're targeting. The way you write an ad for a 25-year-old who just bought their first home is completely different from how you speak to a retired 65-year-old. They may both need HVAC services, but what motivates each of them to buy is not remotely the same.

The same is true when you're selling to both men and women. Husbands and wives often approach buying decisions from completely different emotional drivers. The messaging that lands with a mom making a purchase for her kids is very different from what will motivate a dad making the same purchase. Most entrepreneurs completely miss this level of nuance. That's why their marketing feels generic—and gets ignored.

You learn these nuances by doing the up-front work: focus groups, customer interviews, and market research. When you truly understand your buyer's pain and desires at this level, everything you create—your ads, your emails, your sales videos—becomes laser-focused on delivering exactly what they're looking for.

Because, at the end of the day, that's all we're really selling: outcomes that solve real pain for real people. The more precisely you know your buyer, the easier it is to deliver that solution.

STEP 4: CHANNEL AND PLATFORM STRATEGY

Once you've nailed your buyer persona, your next advantage comes from knowing exactly where to reach them. The more precise your buyer knowledge, the easier it becomes to apply that insight across every marketing channel you use.

The mistake most business owners make is they try to be everywhere, posting everything to everyone. But not every platform is the same, and not every buyer hangs out in the same places.

If you're selling B2B services, LinkedIn may be your primary channel. If you're running consumer offers, Facebook and Instagram often give you better reach. If you're selling visual products like design or fashion, Pinterest might dominate. If you're targeting younger buyers with entertainment-driven content, TikTok could outperform everything else.

For example, I've personally seen my content perform 10 times better on TikTok than on Instagram for the exact same topic. I don't overthink why—I follow the data. If TikTok is pulling the audience I want, that's where I invest more attention.

You need to treat this like channel selection in traditional media. If you're selling golf products, you run ads during Golf Channel broadcasts. If you're selling home decor, you advertise on HGTV. The same logic applies to your digital strategy. You tailor both your platform selection and your content style to the platform where your buyer actually lives.

Even inside the platforms, your content needs to be adapted. A TikTok video requires a strong hook in the first three to five seconds to stop the scroll. Your Instagram stories may be more visual and polished. Your LinkedIn posts will be more professional and authority-driven. You're not just pushing content everywhere. You're tailoring your message for each specific audience segment.

In some cases, you'll have two or three buyer personas inside your business. That's fine. Build them. Put them into a simple Venn diagram. Where they overlap is your sweet spot—the content that resonates with all three. But outside of that overlap, you still speak to each group differently based on who they are, how they think, and where they live online.

STEP 5: CREATE URGENCY AND EXCLUSIVITY

Now let's add fuel to your marketing fire. If you want to create premium pricing and demand, you have to create urgency and exclusivity.

Urgency means there's a limited time to act. The offer closes. The cart shuts down. The bonus disappears. People hate missing out. And deadlines drive decisions.

Exclusivity means not everyone gets access. Scarcity increases perceived value. When access feels limited, buyers lean in faster. That's why elite clubs, VIP lists, private masterminds, and members-only programs can charge dramatically more.

And don't be afraid to make it a little harder to get access. People actually place higher value on offers that feel private or exclusive. That's how you separate serious buyers from browsers, and that's where your premium pricing power lives.

STEP 6: SELL THE OUTCOME, NOT THE PRODUCT

At the end of the day, people do not buy products. They buy outcomes. They are not choosing to book a vacation rental because of the square footage or the furniture. They are buying the experience and the feeling they have when they leave.

That emotional outcome is what you are really selling. When you understand that, your marketing becomes more powerful. The stronger the outcome you deliver, the stronger your message becomes, and the more pricing power you can command.

STEP 7: RESEARCH WHAT YOUR COMPETITORS AREN'T DOING

One of your greatest opportunities for marketing is hiding in plain sight. It is in the gaps your competitors ignore.

Most businesses copy each other. They use the same offers, copy the same marketing, and follow the same pricing models. That creates a huge opportunity for you to do what they're not doing.

Study your competition closely. Look for the pain points they don't solve. Pay attention to the frustrations their customers still complain about. Identify where you can add convenience, access, or experience that nobody else is offering.

Take Delta Air Lines. For years, the industry standard was mediocrity with long delays, miserable customer service, and endless nickel-and-diming. Delta leaned into the gaps. They doubled down on on-time performance, invested in better in-flight experience, and built a loyalty program travelers actually loved. While United and others were apologizing for disasters, Delta marketed reliability and consistency. And passengers noticed . . . including me.

Now, I'm a **1K Premier member with United**—their highest tier in their loyalty program. On paper, United has my business. But after a few recent trips, I've been second-guessing that loyalty. Why? Multiple long delays. No updates or communication. No apologies. No "make good." Nothing. When you're one of their highest-value customers and they can't even acknowledge your time matters, that's a glaring gap you could drive a 737 through.

And that's the point. Find what everyone else accepts as "normal," and refuse to accept it. Fix what nobody else is fixing. Be willing to take the Two Extra Steps. Then market it so clearly that customers can't unsee the difference. That's how you create separation and dominate your category.

YOUR CONTENT CREATION SYSTEM

Once you've built out your Problems and Solutions Worksheet, you don't need to overthink your content strategy. If you've identified five clear problems with corresponding solutions, you already have your first five Facebook ads, your first five LinkedIn posts, and your first five TikTok videos.

From there, you simply let the market guide you. Pay attention to the feedback that comes in, both positive and negative. The comments, the DMs, the reactions—that's your content engine. Use it to shape posts six, seven, eight, nine, and ten. You aren't guessing anymore. You're letting the audience tell you where to go next.

And when you run out of ideas? You don't brainstorm in a vacuum. You go right back to your customer base, to your focus group, to your best buyers. They will tell you what they're struggling with. And that gives you the next round of content.

THE STACKING EFFECT

This is where you should really start to see how all the pieces we've covered in this book begin to stack.

- It starts with your buyer persona.
- Then moves into your value propositions.
- Then into pricing elasticity.
- Then into marketing and positioning.
- Then into your specific problems and solutions.

The constant that runs through it all is uniqueness. You must have something unique to sell and you must be selling an outcome. That's the common thread that makes the whole system work.

THE GOLDEN TICKET

The final piece that ties it all together is confidence.

I cannot stress this enough: You must exude confidence in your marketing—especially when you're selling premium. At every touchpoint, from your Facebook ad copy to your Instagram videos to your in-person conversations, your confidence must come through.

Because when people feel your confidence, they trust you. When you layer that confidence with genuine connection—speaking directly to your buyer's problems, desires, and outcomes—you become unstoppable.

That is your golden ticket. The Willy Wonka moment. Grab it. Hold it with a kung fu death grip. Confidence plus connection is what separates your Super product, your Super service, your Super business from everyone else who's simply posting features and hoping for the best.

THE TWO EXTRA STEPS MARKETING ADVANTAGE

While your competition:

- Markets features and benefits instead of outcomes
- Competes on price instead of value
- Makes their products easily accessible to everyone
- Focuses on operations instead of revenue-driving activities
- Uses the same generic message for every buyer
- Avoids agitating pain points that drive urgency

You will:

- Build unique value propositions that your competition cannot copy
- Leverage urgency and exclusivity to drive demand
- Focus the majority of your time on sales, marketing, and growth
- Agitate pain points to create desire for your solution
- Tailor your message to each buyer persona you serve
- Sell outcomes, transformations, and feelings—not just products

That is how your marketing transforms from ordinary into extraordinary. Where the right combination of small, deliberate moves multiplies your results. Slight differences in how you position, package, and promote your product don't just add up—they compound into pricing power, customer loyalty, and market leadership.

Because the truth is, in today's crowded marketplace, the best product rarely wins. The most visible product wins. The most memorable product wins. The product that creates desire, urgency, and a sense of exclusivity wins. And that is all marketing. When you build something unique and then market it with absolute clarity and confidence, you stop chasing customers and customers start chasing you.

Chapter 8

BUYER JOURNEY AND SALES LADDER

Everything we've covered up to this point leads here.

You've built something unique. You've priced it with confidence. You've positioned it for premium buyers. You've created marketing that focuses on outcomes, not features. You've dialed in what makes your product different, valuable, and desirable.

But now comes the part that separates amateurs from pros: understanding *how* your customers actually buy.

Because here's the truth most business owners miss: You are not in control of your sales process. Your customer is. No matter how perfectly you map out your funnel, people are still going to move at their own pace, follow their own triggers, and make decisions on their own timeline.

If you don't understand the buyer's journey, you'll waste time trying to force people into your process, instead of building a system that meets them exactly where they are.

This is where the real leverage lives. Once you master how your buyer moves—what they need at each stage, what questions they have, what pain they're feeling—you stop guessing. You start building systems that convert naturally. Sales feel easy because your process aligns with how they actually want to buy.

That's what this chapter is about. First, we're going to break down the buyer's journey. Then, I'll show you how to structure your *ascension ladder* so you're giving every buyer a clear, frictionless path to move up and spend more with you over time.

Once you've built both, then you're ready to pull it all together with *smarketing*—where your sales, marketing, and retention teams finally work as one unified revenue machine.

THE THREE-STAGE BUYER'S JOURNEY

There are only three stages to every buyer's journey. Once you lock this in, everything else becomes easier.

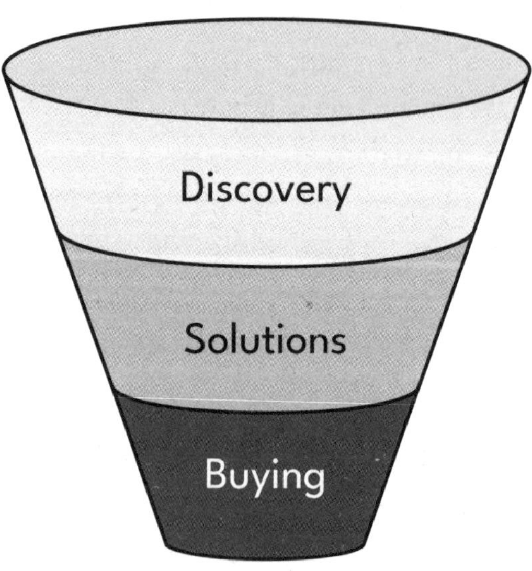

STAGE 1: DISCOVERY (TOP OF FUNNEL)

At this stage, your prospect doesn't fully trust you yet. They're looking for options. They're doing research. They're trying to figure out: "Who can I even trust to solve this?"

Your only job right now is to earn trust. You do that by solving their very first pain point. You connect. You become likable. You show them you understand their problem even better than they do. That starts to separate you from everybody else who's just pitching features.

This is where that first set of hash marks from your Problems and Solutions Worksheet comes in. You meet them at their pain, you show that you have a solution, and you start the relationship.

STAGE 2: SOLUTIONS (MIDDLE OF FUNNEL)

Now they know you exist. They're not just looking for options anymore. They're looking for the best solution.

This is where you go deeper. You're stacking value propositions. You're stacking those pain points and solutions. You're taking them from sad face to happy face like we talked about earlier. You're proving to them why you're different, why you're better, and why you're worth more.

This is where the relationship gets built. This is where they start to picture themselves working with you, buying from you, or joining your program.

STAGE 3: BUYING (BOTTOM OF FUNNEL)

Now they're ready. This is the part where most businesses screw it up.

When your buyer is ready to buy, you better be ready to let them buy. This is why you need a sales process that's flexible. Some buyers want to talk. Some don't. Your sales reps need to know when to:

- Move a buyer straight to the website and let them close themselves
- Deliver a proposal if that's what they need
- Skip the proposal and go directly to contract

If your buyer is ready to go, don't slow them down. That hesitation costs sales every single day.

WHY YOU NEED TO LET YOUR CUSTOMER DRIVE

Earlier, I told you the story about helping my mother-in-law buy a Ford Explorer and how eliminating the painful parts of the process completely changed the experience. That wasn't just about saving time. It was about flipping the script on who controls the transaction.

This is the part most salespeople get wrong. You're not controlling the sales process—they are.

The customer decides how they want to buy. Your job is to make sure your process is flexible enough to meet them wherever they are in that journey.

Think about why the traditional car-buying experience is so awful. You walk in. You know what you want. You know what it costs. And yet, they still make you sit there for hours. You wait for the salesperson. Then finance. Then paperwork. They control the timing. They control the flow. And you leave frustrated.

Don't do that to your customers.

Design your process so the customer feels in control the entire time. Some want to move fast. Some need to ask a million questions. Some need to think about it. Some are ready to buy right now. Let them.

It's not a sales process anymore. It's a buying process. It's their journey, not yours. And the easier you make it for people to buy the way they want to buy, the more deals you'll close without feeling like you're "selling."

When you structure your business around how people actually want to buy, that's where the ascension ladder comes in.

The goal isn't to shove everyone through the same rigid funnel. The goal is to give customers multiple natural ways to move up the ladder at their own pace. Some will move fast. Some will take their time. But if you've built the ladder right, every step feels easy, logical, and frictionless.

Let me show you how that works.

THE SALES LADDER FRAMEWORK: YOUR ASCENSION MODEL

Every great business that scales understands one simple truth: Not every buyer wants to buy the same way. That's why you need what I call an ascension ladder.

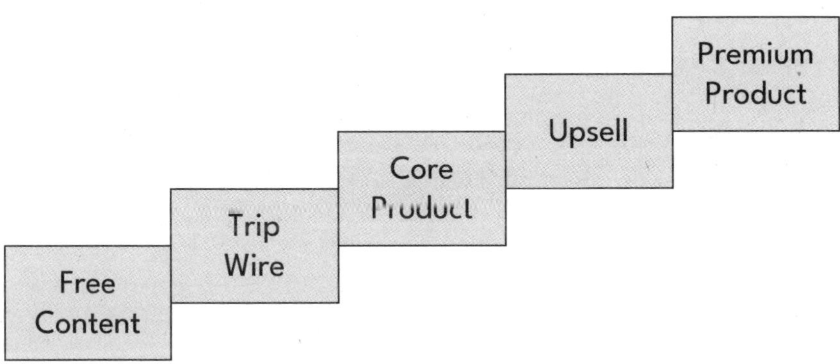

The ascension ladder creates multiple entry points for different types of buyers, but all roads lead to the top. Your best customers naturally climb higher because you've built a system that makes it easy for them to do so.

Here are the five steps.

STEP 1: FREE CONTENT

This is where the relationship starts. Social media, podcasts, YouTube, blog posts, free PDFs. Anything that lets people discover you without pulling out their wallet.

STEP 2: TRIP WIRE

A small, low-risk purchase that moves them from follower to buyer. It might be a $7 e-book, a $27 mini-course, or a $49 resource. The price doesn't matter. The point is to create momentum.

STEP 3: CORE PRODUCT

This is your main offer. The thing you're known for. It solves a real problem and delivers meaningful value. For some buyers, this is as far as they'll go and that's fine.

STEP 4: UPSELL

Once they've bought your core product, you present your next-level solution. This might be advanced training, a done-for-you service, or deeper coaching. They've already raised their hand. Now you're simply offering more value.

STEP 5: PREMIUM PRODUCT

This is your top tier. Your high-ticket, highly personalized, limited-access offer that delivers transformational results for your best clients. Not everyone will make it here. But the ones who do create the biggest revenue and longest retention.

Now here's where most people screw this up. They think buyers need to go through every step in perfect order. That's not how real buying works.

Some customers don't want to waste time. They know what they want, they trust you, and they're ready to go all in immediately. You need to have your ladder built in a way that allows those people to bypass the steps and ascend directly to your premium offer without having to jump through hoops.

The job of your system is simple: Remove friction. Make it easy for every type of buyer to move forward at their pace, not yours.

WHEN THE SALES LADDER WORKS EXACTLY LIKE IT'S SUPPOSED TO

Let me give you a real-world example of how this plays out when you build your system right.

When I first launched my Build Short-Term Rental Wealth mastermind, I handpicked 20 people to invite. This was my first product, first launch. I didn't even really know if anyone would say yes. But I knew who was active in my Facebook group, who was asking questions, who was showing up.

One of those people was Lori. She's one of my OGs.

Now here's where it gets interesting. Lori didn't need a pitch. She didn't need a sales call. She didn't need a webinar. She didn't need me walking her through anything. She went through the entire sales ladder—free content, trip wire, core offer, upsell, straight into the high-ticket mastermind—all on her own. And she did it in less than an hour.

I talked to her about it later, and she just laughed. She said, "Bill, I don't f*** around. When I know, I know. I saw what I needed, and I was in."

That right there is where most of you screw it up. You think everyone needs to be pushed through some long, complicated sales process. Schedule a call. Wait for a demo. Send a proposal. Chase them down. Meanwhile, your buyer is sitting there thinking, *If you'd just let me give you my damn credit card, I'd already be a customer.*

You cannot force people to move at your pace. You have to build your system so they can move at their pace. If I had required Lori to schedule a call or sit through a presentation, I might've lost her. She was ready to buy right now. My job was to get out of her way and let her do it.

That's what your sales ladder needs to be built for. Not just the people who need handholding, but also the buyers who don't f*** around and are ready to ascend right now.

TWO EXTRA STEPS IN ACTION

While your competition:

- Tries to force every customer into one rigid sales funnel
- Assumes everyone needs a full demo or sales call before buying
- Slows down buyers who are ready to buy right now
- Ignores how different buyers want to move at different speeds
- Builds sales processes for their business, not for their customer
- Misses revenue by creating unnecessary friction at every step

You will:

- Design a sales system that meets every buyer exactly where they are
- Give buyers multiple ways to ascend naturally through your offers
- Let fast buyers move quickly without getting in their way
- Build trust and remove friction at every stage of the journey
- Create simple, logical steps that make buying feel easy
- Close more sales by adapting to how people actually want to buy

This is how you transform your sales process into a buying process. One that works with your customer's psychology instead of fighting against it. You are no longer forcing people to follow your path. You are building a system where every buyer finds their own fastest path to saying yes.

And once you have your buyer journey and ascension ladder built, you are ready for the next stage. Because now you're not just selling . . . you're ready to unify sales and marketing into one complete revenue machine. And that's exactly where we're going next with smarketing.

Chapter 9

SMARKETING

Here's why most businesses hit a wall: because sales, marketing, and customer retention operate like three separate islands. The sales team has their little system. Marketing is off running ads and posting social content. Retention is left scrambling to keep customers happy when sales overpromise and marketing sets the wrong expectations.

There's no coordination. No feedback loop. No shared information. And when that happens, you stall. Leads don't convert like they should. Salespeople waste time chasing bad leads. Marketing keeps spending on the wrong messaging. Retention burns out cleaning up the mess.

This is dumb business. It's why so many companies stay small forever.

But when you get this part right—when you align sales, marketing, and retention into one unified system—that's when things start compounding. Because while your competition is managing handoffs between disconnected teams, you're building one seamless customer journey where everything works together:

- Marketing feeds qualified leads into sales.
- Sales closes deals based on real pain points, not hype.

- Retention already knows what was sold and delivers exactly what was promised.
- And everyone's working from the same playbook, every single day.

SMARKETING

Back when I was building one of my earlier businesses, probably around 2008 or 2009, I came across this term while working with HubSpot. Dan Tyre, who was one of the early guys at HubSpot, called it **smarketing**. Sales and marketing combined. Smart marketing.

And let me tell you: Most business owners still don't get what that really means.

Most of you have dumb marketing and dumb sales. I say that with love, but it's true. You hire a social media manager to handle your "marketing," then you've got a sales guy or two trying to close deals, and none of them ever talk to each other. No communication. No alignment. Two totally separate silos doing their own thing. That's not smarketing. That's just dumb.

Smarketing is when sales, marketing, and even customer retention are all locked in together. They are breathing the same air, rowing in the same direction, talking to each other every single day. That's how you scale.

But what happens instead? You put your sales team over here. Your marketing department in another room. Account managers and retention somewhere else. They're all playing their own little games, running separate plays. And you wonder why your growth stalls out.

I believe they should be fully intertwined. They should be having lunch together. They should be talking on breaks. They should be reviewing the same leads and campaigns, together. Because the one thing that ties all of this together—the glue—is your sales and marketing process.

And most businesses don't even have that. Even once they hire a salesperson, they just cut 'em loose: "Go network. Go close people." But there's no actual process. No system.

That's where this starts. If you want real smarketing, you need a defined sales process first. Every lead that comes in should be tracked from the source. That goes straight into your CRM—Pipedrive, Salesforce, HubSpot, or what I recommend for most small businesses: Go High Level.

Go High Level gives you everything in one place. CRM, email marketing, text marketing, calendar appointments, the whole thing. It's like a scaled-down HubSpot without the big price tag. And it works.

YOUR SMARKETING SYSTEM: THE COMPLETE FRAMEWORK

Now that you get the point of smarketing—sales and marketing fully aligned, working together, not running around like two separate dumb departments—let's talk about how you actually build it.

Because most small businesses? They don't have a sales process. Hell, they barely have a marketing process. They hire a salesperson, tell them to "go network" or "go sell," hire some kid to do social media, and then wonder why revenue's stuck. That's dumb. And that's exactly why we're fixing it right now.

STEP 1: DEFINE YOUR SALES PROCESS FIRST

You have to build the sales foundation before marketing can even help you. Here's your baseline:

- Lead comes in—source must be tracked.
- It gets entered into your CRM—I don't care which one: Pipedrive, Salesforce, HubSpot, Go High Level.
- Then you build automated workflows: email, text, video follow-ups, voice drops, whatever you can automate to make sure nobody falls through the cracks.

For 99% of small businesses, I recommend Go High Level. It's like HubSpot's little brother that actually knows you don't have a Fortune 500 budget. They have:

- CRM
- Email marketing
- Text marketing
- Calendar appointments
- Everything

STEP 2: LEARN HOW YOUR CUSTOMERS WANT TO BE SOLD TO

Don't sit in a room and make this up. That's what dumb businesses do. They make up some complicated sales process and force buyers to jump through hoops. You need to go talk to your customers.

Here's your action item: Take 10 of your happiest customers. Ask them:

- When you bought from us, what could we have done better or faster?
- What frustrated you?
- What would've made you spend more?
- Where could we have offered you more services or higher-level offers?

They'll literally hand you the sales process they wish you had built. That's how you learn how your customers want to buy, not how you want to sell.

STEP 3: CREATE YOUR OBJECTION LIBRARY

One of the most powerful tools your sales team will ever have is your objection library. You gather every objection your team hears—whether it's from sales calls, emails, retention calls—and you write out the best answers.

Store it everywhere:

- On every sales rep's screen
- Inside your CRM
- On Google Drive or Dropbox
- On their phones before every sales meeting

And you prioritize them by how often they come up. This way, your reps are never caught flat-footed again.

STEP 4: MASTER THE FIRST 90 SECONDS

The first 30 to 90 seconds of every sales conversation will make or break the entire deal. Period. Most salespeople screw this up because they jump straight into pitching. They start rattling off features, prices, and benefits before they've even earned the right to have that conversation.

That's not how you sell. That's how you chase people away.

Here's the truth: In those first 90 seconds, your only job is to lower their guard. You're not closing. You're not pitching. You're not trying to convince them of anything yet. You are disarming them.

- Build trust: Make them feel like you're here to serve, not sell.
- Make a personal connection: Find something you have in common. Use their first name. Acknowledge why they're here. Make it feel like a conversation, not a transaction.
- Ask questions: Open-ended questions that get them talking about their situation, their goals, their problems.
- Shut up and listen: When they start talking, you stop talking. Let them tell you exactly what they need and where their pain points are.

Because here's what happens: Once people feel safe, they'll open up. They'll tell you exactly what they want. They'll literally hand you the road map to closing them. You just have to listen for it. And once they feel heard? Once they feel like you actually get it? That's when they're ready to buy. That's when you can move them into your solution.

If you nail those first 90 seconds, your close rate will go through the roof. You'll find yourself doing one-call closes over and over again because you're not forcing the sale. You're guiding them to a decision they already want to make.

STEP 5: USE PATTERN INTERRUPTS

At some point, you're going to hear it:

"Well, I need to talk to my spouse."

Or:

"I'm just not ready to make a decision today."

Or:

"I need to think about it."

That's the stall. And if you let them get away with that, they're gone. They walk out, and nine times out of ten, they don't come back.

This is where you need a pattern interrupt.

A pattern interrupt is simply breaking their mental loop. They're falling into a script—one they've probably used before to delay or avoid making a decision. You're not going to argue with them. You're not going to push. You're just going to snap them out of that pattern for a second.

It might sound like:

"Wait, you need to talk to your spouse? Is it because you wore those bright red shoes today and you don't feel comfortable making decisions in those things?"

Now, obviously, they'll pause. They might be confused or laugh awkwardly. They'll likely say, "What? No."

That's your opening. You've broken the pattern. You've shifted the conversation out of their well-rehearsed excuse and back into real dialogue. And once you've done that, you can circle back . . .

"Look, totally get it. But let's be honest . . . Based on everything we just talked about, is this really about needing more time, or are you just not 100% sold yet? If there's something you're still unsure about, let's address it now while we're both here."

You've brought them back into the conversation. You're showing confidence, but without being aggressive. This is how you keep control of the sales process without creating pressure.

The pattern interrupt isn't about being slick or cute. It's about keeping momentum. It's about not letting objections derail a close that was already on track.

STEP 6: CONFIRM DECISION-MAKING AUTHORITY

Right up front, usually in that first 90 seconds, you need to confirm who you are talking to. Are they actually the one who can say yes? Are they decisive? Are they an action taker?

And trust me, they will all say yes in the beginning. Everybody wants to believe they are the decision-maker. So you lock that in early while they are still excited and engaged. It might sound like this: "Just so I know before we dive in, if this makes sense, are you the one who can make the call today?"

If they say yes, perfect. Now you have something to anchor to later. So when you get to the close and they start with the stalls like "I need to think about it" or "I need to talk to someone," you can confidently bring them back.

"Totally understand, but earlier you told me you were the one who could make the call. Has something changed, or is there something we need to clear up right now?"

This is how you eliminate stalls and get to the close faster. If you can get them to admit they are the action taker early, your one-call close percentage will skyrocket.

STEP 7: ALIGN MARKETING TO SUPPORT SALES

This is why you always start by defining your sales process first. Because once that's in place, your marketing team knows exactly what to build around.

Their job is simple: Take everything you are using in sales and turn it into marketing fuel.

They need to know:

- What objections your sales team hears every day
- What solutions you offer to those objections
- What pain points you are solving at each stage

Every single one of those can become a marketing asset. If you have one objection, you don't just answer it once. You build four, five, even six pieces of content around it. Video. Email. Paid ads. Social posts. Webinar slides. All of it.

The mistake most companies make is sales and marketing never talk to each other. Sales hears all the real-world objections and pain points, but marketing keeps creating generic top-of-funnel fluff that doesn't actually support closing deals.

When sales and marketing are fully aligned, marketing isn't guessing anymore. They are simply amplifying and pre-solving what sales already knows moves people to buy.

STEP 8: TRACK AND OPTIMIZE YOUR PIPELINE

Look, this is not a set-it-and-forget-it system. Your pipeline will evolve as your customers react, as offers change, and as your team gets better. That's exactly why you have to track everything.

You need to know:

- What percentage of customers are closing at each stage of your funnel
- How much revenue each stage is producing
- Where the bottlenecks actually live

Because once you have that data, you can make real decisions.

For example, let's say you're tracking your proposals. You find out that Dave is closing 67% of his proposals, but Bill is only closing 32%. Well, guess what? Dave doesn't need to be doing anything else. Get him off all the other stuff and let him run proposals full-time. That's how you optimize.

This is how you turn your sales and marketing process into one unified revenue machine.

When you do this right, you now have your sales team, your marketing team, and your client retention team all aligned. They're operating with:

- The same goals
- The same messaging
- The same objections and solutions
- The same customer journey

TWO EXTRA STEPS IN ACTION

While your competition:

- Runs sales, marketing, and retention like three separate silos
- Has no feedback loop between what sales hears and what marketing creates
- Forces buyers through rigid sales funnels that don't match how people actually want to buy
- Leaves sales teams flying blind without an objection library or clear process

- Lets weak salespeople waste leads instead of optimizing around what actually closes
- Creates content that feels disconnected from real buying conversations

You will:

- Build one unified system where sales, marketing, and retention operate from the same playbook
- Align your messaging, content, and sales process around real objections and solutions
- Empower your best salespeople to focus on the parts of the pipeline where they close best
- Equip every sales rep with a library of objections and pattern interrupts that keep deals moving
- Let buyers control their path, while still guiding them toward higher-ticket offers
- Track every stage of your pipeline so you know exactly where money is being won or lost

That is how smarketing becomes your compounding advantage.

Because while most businesses are still playing a game of disconnected handoffs, you've built one seamless customer journey that converts faster, closes stronger, and compounds revenue at every stage.

Chapter 10

CUSTOMER SERVICE

Customer service these days is a lost art. You call any business and what happens? You sit through a phone tree for five minutes, press option after option, wait on hold forever, and half the time you never even get a real person. And if you finally do, it's someone reading from a script who can't actually help you.

That's not customer service. That's customer avoidance.

And here's where almost every business owner screws it up: They think customer service starts after the sale, like it's some separate department that kicks in once the deal is done. The salesperson closes the deal. Then they hand it off. "Thanks for your money—now go talk to support."

That's dumb business.

Because what the 99% completely miss is this: The minute that contract is signed is when your real opportunity starts. That is when you have the chance to create loyalty, extract more revenue, and turn good customers into lifelong advocates who sell for you. That's where your margin lives. That's where your referrals live. That's where lifetime value multiplies.

The best businesses don't separate sales from service. They turn service into an extension of the sales process. They create world-class experiences that make people feel taken care of every step of the way.

And that's why, for you, customer service won't be a cost center. It's going to become your secret growth engine.

WHEN 87 DAYS CREATES A CUSTOMER FOR LIFE

What comes to mind when you think of exceptional hospitality and customer service? For most people, it's high-end, white-glove treatment.

Maybe you picture something like the Mandarin Oriental—one of the most exclusive luxury hotel brands in the world, with fewer than 40 properties globally. They've built a reputation on precision and personalization. Guests in their Fans of M.O. loyalty program enjoy bespoke perks, and their app lets you manage every element of your stay, from booking to curated experiences, before you even arrive. That level of thoughtfulness is why they're considered one of the top names in boutique luxury.

And yet as impressive as that sounds, the single best example of customer service I've ever experienced didn't happen at the Mandarin Oriental. It happened at the Four Seasons in Boston.

Back when I was scaling businesses and working with HubSpot, I practically lived at the Four Seasons on Boylston Street, right across from Boston Common. For two or three years, that was my second home.

Then life shifted. I stopped traveling to Boston. Two, maybe three years went by without a single stay.

Finally, a board meeting brought me back. I landed at Logan, got picked up by Commonwealth Transportation like always, and walked into the hotel. I hadn't taken more than three steps before I heard:

"Welcome back, Mr. Faeth."

I stopped in my tracks. I looked over at the concierge and said, "What's your name?"

She said, "My name's Cassandra."

I asked, "How long have you worked here?"

"Four and a half years."

"Do you realize I haven't been here in two or three years?"

She smiled. "Oh, I didn't know that."

I pressed a little more. "Then how did you recognize me?"

She hesitated for a second, then explained. "We get reports of returning guests. If we have headshots or any past information, we review them before your arrival. I knew how many nights you had stayed with us."

I asked, "How many nights?"

"Eighty-seven."

"And you knew I was being dropped off?"

"We have security cameras, Mr. Faeth. I saw you get out of the Commonwealth SUV, checked my notes, and was ready to greet you."

That moment made me feel like royalty. Like I mattered. That is the power of Two Extra Steps. That is how you create loyalty that lasts for years. It wasn't about the fancy lobby or the expensive room. It was about the feeling they created before I even reached the front desk.

This is what customer service done right looks like. Personalized. Intentional. Proactive. And, most of all, unforgettable.

HOW I APPLIED IT: MAKING CUSTOMERS FEEL FAMOUS

I applied the same approach when I was scaling my ground transportation company, Silver Oak Transportation.

If you've ever flown into LAX, LaGuardia, or any major airport as a corporate traveler, you know exactly how this usually goes. You get off the escalator and there's a wall of guys in black suits, white shirts, black shoes. Everyone looks the same.

Half of them are holding a wrinkled sheet of paper with your name scribbled in barely legible handwriting. Some have upgraded to an iPad, but it's still completely impersonal. You walk up, they say, "Welcome to New York," or "Welcome to Nashville," and off you go. No connection. No experience.

We took it one step further.

Before a client ever arrived, we would research them on LinkedIn—just like the Four Seasons concierge reviewing guest profiles. And we trained our chauffeurs to deliver a completely different first impression.

At baggage claim, they weren't standing around holding a piece of paper. They were actively scanning for the client's face, ready to step forward the moment they made eye contact. Then came the script . . .

"Mr. Smith, my name is Bill Faeth. I'm with Silver Oak Transportation, and I'll be your chauffeur today. It's such a pleasure to welcome you to Nashville. May I take your bag or assist you with anything?

"Do you have any checked luggage? Great, we'll head to carousel nine. The car is in short-term parking just a few steps away. Once we grab your bags, we'll be on the road and at your hotel in about seven to ten minutes. And if you'd like to make any stops on the way, just let me know. I'm happy to accommodate."

Completely different from the usual robotic pickup.

And you know what we'd hear almost every single time?

"Wow. How did you know who I was?"

That right there is where the magic happens. It makes people feel important. It makes them feel seen. Almost like they're famous. And that feeling is what creates loyalty.

That's taking the Two Extra Steps. That's knowing your buyer before they ever say a word.

400K WON WITH ELF COSTUMES

When I was building my ground transportation company, one of the biggest accounts I ever landed came from a company called Asurion. You probably don't even realize it, but if you've got insurance on your phone, tablet, or laptop, odds are you're using Asurion. They control over 95% of that market.

I had been chasing their business for years. Multiple meetings. Countless emails. No traction. Then one summer they invited us to their vendor day—a Christmas in July event for all their partners. It was our shot to finally make an impression. And we were not about to show up like everybody else.

Fifteen vendors were there: airlines, hotels, rental cars, other ground transportation companies. Most set up boring tables with brochures, candy bowls, and pens. You know the routine.

We didn't do that.

Instead, my business development director, Don England, and I showed up dressed as full-on elves. We hired Shank Photography to set up professional photo booths. We brought in a full Santa Claus setup. Employees could take Christmas photos with Santa and the elves, and we printed and handed out those photos on the spot.

We didn't just hand out flyers. We created an experience. Something people would actually remember.

But that was only part of the play.

The real move? We targeted the six travel managers—the people who actually controlled the booking and vendor relationships for all of Asurion's global ground transportation. These are the ones making decisions for the C-suite, for the sales teams, for the execs. But here's what most people miss: These bookers rarely get to experience the services they're contracting for.

We flipped that on its head.

We created what we called "Executive for a Day." Each travel manager got the full VIP experience:

- Picked up at their home in the morning and chauffeured to the office.
- Picked up at lunch and taken wherever they wanted.
- Picked up after work with two hours of personal service—grocery store, dinner, happy hour, wherever they chose.

For the first time, they experienced our service the same way their executives would. And that changed everything.

Our goal was simple: Get all six of them fully activated and booking rides within the first week of signing the contract. We got five out of six activated immediately. The sixth was on vacation.

But here's the part I'll never forget. Before we even scheduled her "Executive for a Day" ride when she returned, she emailed me:

"I can't wait to experience it for myself. But honestly, after hearing what all my coworkers have said, I've already started booking."

That's how you win business.

That contract was worth over $400,000 a year. And because we shortened the activation window, we didn't leave months of revenue on the table. If we had waited 90 days to fully onboard them like most companies do, that could've been $100,000 to $130,000 lost.

This is the power of customer experience done right. Not just delivering what you promised, but going so far beyond expectation that your customers become your advocates before you've even finished onboarding them.

THE PERSONAL PHONE CALL THAT DROPPED CHURN BY 80%

One of the most powerful customer experience moves I ever made was one of the simplest.

Back at Silver Oak Transportation, we ran into a problem as we started to scale. The sales team would close new clients, then hand them off to the inside account managers for onboarding and ongoing support. On paper, that looks efficient. In reality? It caused churn.

Here's why. When I was personally closing deals early on, I built relationships with those clients. They trusted me. They knew they could call me directly. But as we scaled and I wasn't doing the selling anymore, that personal connection disappeared. Clients felt like they were being passed off to strangers. And when small onboarding hiccups happened—which they always do—they didn't have any emotional loyalty to us yet. Some never even activated. Others would cancel before we barely got started.

The solution was so simple it's almost embarrassing: one phone call.

We implemented a personal call from me into our activation process. Right after implementation was completed but before they started booking rides, I'd pick up the phone and call every new client personally. The call took no more than three to five minutes.

Here's exactly what I would say:

"Hey, John, this is Bill Faeth. I just wanted to personally welcome you to our company. I know you've wrapped up implementation, and I wanted to check in and make sure everything went smooth. More importantly, I want you to know that even though you'll be working with our account team moving forward, you are always welcome to reach out to me directly.

"I'm going to give you my personal cell phone number right now. If you ever run into any issue while traveling or need anything at all, you can call me. You've also got our 800 number, but I want you to have direct access if you ever need it.

"And by the way, your business means a lot to us. I've already upgraded your account to VIP status. That means you now have a priority number that skips the phone tree and routes directly to our senior account managers anytime you need help."

That one tiny gesture—a personal welcome call with direct contact info—changed everything.

- Our churn rate dropped by 80%.
- Our activation time accelerated by 65%.
- We started generating revenue from new clients 65% faster.

This is what I mean when I talk about customer experience being your secret weapon. The big wins often come from the Two Extra Steps your competition is simply too lazy to do.

ANSWER IN TWO RINGS

Let me give you another simple example of how elite customer experience separates you from the pack.

The company that used to pick me up when I'd travel to Boston—Commonwealth Transportation—has had the same policy for over 30 years: They answer the phone in two rings. Every single time.

Their founder, Dawson Rutter, saw one of the biggest frustrations in the transportation industry. Larger companies would either leave you sitting on hold or dump you into a phone tree, where you'd waste 10 minutes pressing buttons before you finally reached a human being.

You've experienced it yourself. Try calling any major bank, airline, or insurance company and watch how long it takes to actually speak to someone. It's painful.

Dawson decided to solve that problem. He made "answer in two rings" a core part of their customer experience. Not just a nice idea—a nonnegotiable company policy. They even track it. They literally time how long it takes for reps to pick up the phone.

It's not complicated. It doesn't cost anything. But it changes how customers feel.

Because when your client calls and hears a live voice immediately, they feel taken care of. They feel like they matter. That's customer experience.

And it's one more example of how small, intentional decisions stack up and create a business that clients never want to leave.

THE AIRBNB WELCOME VIDEO: FIVE MINUTES THAT PREVENT CANCELLATIONS

Earlier in the book, I told you about the personalized welcome videos I send to every Airbnb guest. What I didn't tell you is why that idea was born. It wasn't just about creating a great experience—it started as pure risk mitigation.

When I started applying the Two Extra Steps inside my Airbnb business, I asked myself: "Where are we most vulnerable?" The answer was obvious: the gap between booking and arrival. That's the danger zone. During that window, guests can still cancel. And I don't care how amazing your listing photos are, second-guessing creeps in. Life happens. People reconsider.

So I built a simple, personal touchpoint that eliminates 95% of that risk: a short welcome video recorded on my phone. No script. No editing. Just me. It's personalized for every single guest. And I send it as fast as I can, ideally within five minutes of them booking whenever possible. If I'm on a plane or traveling, it might take an hour or two, but I get it out as quickly as I can. Either way, it goes straight to their phone so it gets seen.

It sounds like this:

"Hi, Ashley, thanks so much for booking [property name]. My name's Bill, my wife's Brea, and we're your personal hosts. We're looking forward to serving you and your family. If you need anything between now and your stay, just reach out. And by the way, I think you're really going to love these three things about the property: [insert three UVPs]."

It's five minutes of my time, but that tiny step does two critical things:

1. It instantly builds trust and personal connection.
2. It dramatically reduces cancellations because now they feel seen, taken care of, and excited.

And I'll tell you right now, it's not always convenient. Half the time it hits while I'm at dinner or in a meeting. But if it's a $20,000 or $30,000 booking? I stop what I'm doing. That five-minute video protects my revenue, protects my calendar, and delivers a level of service 99% of other hosts won't bother to do.

It's customer service, but it's also smart sales. Because every time you make your customer feel special, you don't just keep the booking—you create an advocate.

TWO EXTRA STEPS IN ACTION

While your competition:

- Treats customer service like a cost center that only handles problems
- Hands off new clients with no personal connection or follow-up
- Delays activation with slow, impersonal onboarding
- Makes customers sit through endless phone trees and long hold times
- Offers generic, transactional service that feels robotic and replaceable
- Leaves loyalty and lifetime value entirely to chance

You will:

- Turn customer experience into your most powerful growth engine
- Build personal relationships from day one through simple touchpoints
- Accelerate onboarding and activation with proactive communication
- Make every client feel known, valued, and taken care of at every step
- Create moments that feel like VIP treatment, not just fulfillment
- Stack emotional loyalty that creates long-term retention, referrals, and expansion revenue

That's how your customer experience compounds. Because while everyone else is still playing defense after the sale, you're playing offense. You're using every interaction—before, during, and after the sale—to build deeper trust, stronger relationships, and more revenue without needing to chase new customers every month.

This is where 2 + 2 stops equaling 4. This is where customer service becomes customer growth. This is how you create clients for life.

Chapter 11

ACCELERATE YOUR GROWTH

If you want to scale, you better get this part right: Profitability comes first. Period.

Too many entrepreneurs think they can grow their way into profitability. They believe if they just get big enough, the profit will show up later. That might work for Silicon Valley startups burning through venture capital, but that's not your reality. You don't have a hedge fund writing blank checks. You don't have unlimited rounds of funding. You have your cash flow, and that means profitability has to be built into your business from day one.

This is one of the most common places where small business owners screw it up. They focus on top-line revenue, but ignore the margins. They chase sales instead of focusing on sustainable, scalable profit.

And one of the fastest ways you can start stacking profitability is by getting smarter about your pricing.

MASTERING DYNAMIC PRICING (YOUR REAL-WORLD PRICING ELASTICITY)

We learned earlier about pricing elasticity—how small shifts in your pricing strategy can unlock massive growth. This is where that principle keeps paying off.

Your pricing can't be static. You have to build flexibility into it, just like the biggest industries do. Airlines do it. Hotels do it. Uber does it. Short-term rentals do it. The price moves based on supply and demand because that's how you maximize every single unit of inventory you have.

Dynamic pricing is just pricing elasticity applied in real time. And this applies to far more than SaaS or STRs. I'll give you a simple example. Here in Nashville, we've got some of the best barbecue around—places like Edley's and Martin's.

If you show up after the lunch rush, you're probably not getting brisket. They run out almost every day. And yet, they still charge the same price whether you're first in line at 11 AM or scrambling to grab the last slice at 1 PM.

That's the opportunity they're missing. Dynamic pricing would let them scale their profit like this:

- Before lunch rush: $12.99 a pound.
- As inventory drops during lunch: Raise it a dollar.
- After lunch, with limited brisket left: Bump it another $2.

Small shifts like that do two critical things:

1. Increase profitability automatically—you earn higher margin on the same inventory without any extra overhead.
2. Create urgency—customers start showing up earlier to secure what they want before inventory runs out.

This is pricing elasticity in action. You don't need complicated models. You need to pay attention to buyer behavior. Small adjustments like this start stacking profitability without changing anything about your product. You're simply capturing opportunities your competition ignores.

MARKETING: THE GROWTH MULTIPLIER

We've talked about marketing throughout this book. But when it comes to scaling, marketing becomes your single biggest separator. The businesses that know how to execute world-class marketing and advertising pull away from everyone else. Period.

Most small business owners approach marketing with a scarcity mindset. They try to save their way into growth. They'll say: "*Man, I don't want to hire that agency. I'll run Facebook ads myself. I'll figure it out on YouTube.*"

They tinker around. They dabble. They might even get lucky and spend $500 a month. But they never push to $600. Or $1,000. Or $5,000. They plateau before they ever give themselves a chance to scale. And when they don't see results fast enough, they convince themselves it doesn't work. They pull the plug. And they stay small.

My mindset is simple: *Go all in or don't bother.*

Over the last 10 to 12 years, I've spent more than $16 million on ads across Google, Facebook, TikTok, Snapchat, LinkedIn—you name it. And I don't run my own ads anymore. I hire the best people in the world to run them for me.

When I first sat down with Nikki, the owner of the agency who helped scale Codie Sanchez's brand (you might know her book *Main Street Millionaire*), she asked me the same question every agency asks: "*What's your starting ad budget?*"

I didn't hesitate: "*Let's start at $5,000. But I want to get to $50,000 as fast as we can.*"

That's the difference. Most people want to "see what happens" with

$5K. I'm planning from day one how to get to $50K. Because I know—and Nikki knows—that the person who can spend the most money to acquire customers wins.

Going all in doesn't mean you're reckless. It means you're aggressive *and* smart. And yes, you still have to track everything. Here's exactly what I track constantly:

- Return on ad spend (ROAS)
- Weekly profitability
- Sales team close rates
- Conversion rates from ad to sales call
- No-show rates on sales calls
- Conversion rates per sales rep
- Average time to close a deal
- Lifetime customer value
- Cost per call booked
- Cost per conversion (for both sales calls and direct purchases)

Most small business owners don't track any of this. So they don't know what's actually working. They can't diagnose what's broken. And when they don't know, they assume marketing doesn't work. They give up. They never take the Two Extra Steps.

THE TWO EXTRA STEPS THAT ACCELERATE GROWTH

- Hire experts who know how to scale ads.
- Spend aggressively once you find proof of return.
- Track your numbers like your business depends on it—because it does.

This is exactly how you pull away from your competition while they're still stuck debating whether or not they can "afford" to spend more than $500 a month on Facebook.

STRATEGIC PARTNERSHIPS: GET OFF EXILE ISLAND

Most entrepreneurs wait way too long to build the right partnerships. They sit around hoping someone will find them. Meanwhile, they're sitting on Exile Island—all alone, no one to bounce ideas off, no one to challenge their thinking, no one to step in with capital when they hit a ceiling.

And you will hit a ceiling. I've been there.

When I was running Wild Bill's Texas Smokehouse, I remember borrowing from my own savings on a Wednesday to make payroll Friday, then waiting for credit card batches to clear the next Monday to pay it back. If I had brought in a partner early or secured a cash injection, I could have avoided that cycle entirely.

But like many entrepreneurs, my ego got in the way. I wanted to prove I could do it alone. I didn't want to owe anyone. And that nearly cost me more than I realized at the time.

Now? I see partnerships completely differently. The right partnerships give you capital, expertise, relationships, infrastructure: the fuel that allows you to scale faster than you ever could alone.

The key is not waiting until you're desperate. You find partnerships while you still have leverage. That's one of those Two Extra Steps that separates businesses that scale fast from businesses that stall out.

BUILDING COMMUNITY: THE ULTIMATE GROWTH MULTIPLIER

Most people overlook community. But community is one of the greatest compounding advantages you can build.

Look at my friend Pace Morby. He built his real estate education business by building community first. Over 600,000 people now belong to his world—because he focused on giving value, building trust, and creating connection from day one.

When I started Build Short-Term Rental Wealth, I followed the same playbook.

For six full months I had no product, no course, no mastermind. Nothing to sell. I spent five to seven hours a day simply helping people inside Facebook groups, LinkedIn, Clubhouse, Instagram—wherever I could find people to serve.

By the end of that first six months, I had 2,200 people inside my Facebook group. Today? Over 35,000.

And while that may not be the biggest community in the world, it is one of the most engaged, helpful, and supportive you'll find anywhere in the short-term rental world. And those are the people who fill my events, join my programs, and stay with me year after year.

THE TWO EXTRA STEPS:

- Build community *before* product.
- Deliver value long before you ask for the sale. Earn trust before you monetize.

If you do that, you scale faster than everyone who tries to sell first and build trust later.

TWO EXTRA STEPS IN ACTION

While your competition:

- Chases top-line revenue and ignores profitability
- Sets prices once and never adjusts for demand
- Tries to save their way into growth by playing small with marketing
- Waits too long to form partnerships and stays isolated

- Focuses only on selling product and ignores building real community
- Gives up when early growth feels slow or uncomfortable

You will:

- Build profitability into your business from day one
- Use dynamic pricing to maximize margin and create urgency
- Go all in on marketing with aggressive but calculated investment
- Seek out partnerships that accelerate capital, knowledge, and scale
- Build community first, before you ever ask for the sale
- Stack small advantages layer after layer until growth compounds

This is where growth accelerates. Not because you did one thing right, but because you consistently took Two Extra Steps in every area where others cut corners. And when you stack those small advantages, you don't just outgrow your competition—you leave them wondering how you pulled so far ahead.

Chapter 12

LEADERSHIP AND TEAM SCALING

You don't just run your business. You lead it.

That means you protect it. You guide it. You take full ownership for everything that happens inside of it. And you stay ready to adapt when the market shifts, the people shift, and the problems show up—because they always will.

This is where most business owners get stuck. They think leadership is about revenue. Or about making big decisions. Or hiring a few people and barking out orders. But that's not leadership. That's playing boss.

Real leadership is two things:

- Radical accountability inside your walls
- Market adaptability outside your walls

You've got to take ownership first at the micro level, where 99% of problems start—inside your business. Then, as you scale, you have to stay flexible enough to pivot when the market moves on you.

Let's start with the one thing most business owners avoid first: taking radical accountability.

THE BUCK STOPS WITH YOU

Here's the truth nobody wants to hear: **It's always your fault.**

If something goes wrong in your business, it doesn't matter who made the mistake. Doesn't matter which employee messed up. Doesn't matter who dropped the ball. At the end of the day, you own the outcome.

When something goes wrong, too many business owners try to shift blame. They point fingers. They pass problems off to staff or hide behind policy. That instinct right there? That's what destroys businesses. Not just because customers get frustrated, but because your employees lose respect for you too.

The truth is simple: Every win belongs to your team. Every failure belongs to you.

That's leadership. You celebrate your people when things go right, but you absorb the hits when they go wrong. And how you handle those moments—when things break, customers are upset, or mistakes get made—is exactly what separates average leaders from great ones.

Let me give you a simple example.

THE STEAK HOUSE STORY: FOUR LEVELS OF LEADERSHIP

You go out for a nice dinner. You order a $50 steak, medium rare. It comes out well done. Completely wrong. Now watch how four different levels of leadership handle the exact same situation.

LEVEL 1: THE SERVER

The server apologizes, grabs your plate, takes it back to the kitchen. Twenty-five minutes later, your replacement steak shows up. Nobody says anything else. Your dinner's delayed, everyone else at your table is done eating, and you still pay full price. You leave annoyed. You don't complain, but you probably don't come back.

LEVEL 2: COMP THE STEAK

Same situation, but this time, the server takes the steak off the bill. It's better. You're less frustrated. But the overall experience still feels like a miss. You probably still tell a few friends about it and not in a good way.

LEVEL 3: THE MANAGER

Now the manager steps in. They apologize, comp the steak, bring desserts for the entire table, and acknowledge how frustrating the situation was. That changes your whole feeling about the night. You feel seen. You feel valued. Now you're more likely to return because of how they handled the mistake.

LEVEL 4: THE OWNER (THIS IS TWO EXTRA STEPS LEADERSHIP)

Here's where the difference maker lives. The owner comes out, pulls up a chair, and sits down next to you.

"My name's Bob. I've owned this restaurant for 17 years. First of all, I'm mortified this happened. My chef has been with me seven years, trained in France—he knows better. But this one's on me. We're going to get to the bottom of it so it never happens again. Tonight, your entire meal is on the house. Desserts are coming out for the whole table. And I just want you to know how much we appreciate your business."

How do you feel now?

You're not just a customer anymore. You feel like part of the family. And that restaurant? It just went from a place you eat to a place you tell everyone about. That's what Two Extra Steps looks like inside customer experience.

This is what great leadership does. Most owners operate at Level 1 or 2. Good ones make it to Level 3. But the ones who build real loyalty. Who build businesses that thrive for decades. They're the ones who consistently lead at Level 4.

That's where you need to live.

RADICAL ACCOUNTABILITY INSIDE YOUR TEAM

What I just showed you with the steak house? That same principle applies inside your company too. Because here's where most owners screw this up: They take responsibility for customers, but they don't take responsibility for their team.

When your employees drop the ball, when your managers make bad calls, when your staff creates problems that shouldn't exist: Guess what? That's still on you.

You hired them. You trained them (or didn't). You built the system they're operating inside. If they're failing, it's because—somewhere upstream—leadership failed first. And leadership means you.

Now here's the nuance most business owners miss. Great leaders absorb blame, but they don't carry excuses.

You don't excuse poor performance. You don't coddle people who aren't executing. You hold your team to a high standard. But you also recognize that if they're struggling, you have to own the root cause. Are they in the wrong seat? Are they undertrained? Are your expectations clear? Are your processes broken?

When you own that, your team sees it. And ironically, that's what earns their loyalty and performance. Not fear. Not threats. But the knowledge that you've got their back and you're serious about building something great together.

If you want 2 + 2 to start adding up to 5, this is one of the biggest mindset shifts you have to make. You're not just responsible for what happens. You're responsible for what allowed it to happen.

THE LEADERSHIP & MANAGEMENT EVOLUTION

I'll be the first to admit . . . I didn't get this right for a long time.

For years, I was great at being the entrepreneur, the big vision guy, the closer. But when it came to management? I was a disaster. And I didn't even realize there was a difference.

To me, leadership and management were the same thing. Lead the company. Drive the sales. Push people hard. If someone couldn't keep up? Replace them. I treated employees like parts in a machine. And when they broke or burned out, I just found new parts.

And yeah, for a while that worked. We made money. We grew. But underneath it all, there was constant churn. No real loyalty. The culture was fragile. Every time I tried to scale, it would break.

The shift came when I started working with my mentor, John Bearden. John looked me straight in the eye and said, "Bill, you're not a bad leader. You're a bad manager. And until you fix that, you'll never build the kind of company you actually want."

That hit me like a brick. Because what he showed me was this:

- Leadership is vision, values, and direction.
- Management is structure, clarity, and consistency.
- And both are your responsibility.

The moment I stopped ruling through fear, stopped treating employees like they were disposable, and actually invested in my people—everything changed.

I started hiring differently. I learned who they were as human beings, not just employees. I started DiSC profiling every hire. I cared more about getting them in the right seat than squeezing more work out of them. And, most importantly, I finally built a real leadership team that could scale with me.

We tripled revenue. I pulled myself out of the weeds. And I finally had people I could trust running the business alongside me. All because I stopped trying to just be the boss, and learned how to be a true leader and manager.

BE FIRST IN, LAST OUT

Leadership isn't just about what you say. It's what you model. Your team watches everything you do and they take their cues from you.

If you're the first one in every morning, they notice that. If you're the one who takes out the trash when it needs to be done, they notice that. If you're willing to clean a bathroom, they damn sure notice that.

Here's what it looks like when you screw it up royally.

I sold one of my companies to a gentleman about 15 years ago, and we built this brand-new, amazing facility. There was an executive wing that you had to have a key card to get into. Only the executives were allowed in that side of the office.

He'd roll in around nine or ten every morning in his $250,000 Mercedes-AMG and park it right in the very first spot by the front door so everybody could see it. Every single day. Then he'd leave by two o'clock. First in? Not even close. Last out? Never.

How do you think that made the staff feel?

Turnover shot through the roof. We lost 120 to 130% of the staff in the first 12 months after that acquisition. And it wasn't because people couldn't do the job—it was because they no longer believed in who they were following.

That's the difference.

The right way? You stay accessible. You stay humble. You stay involved. You're not hiding behind a closed-door office while your people are in the trenches. You lead by example. You show your people that you're in it with them.

And when the shit hits the fan? You take the hit. Even if it wasn't your direct fault, it rolls uphill. Always.

You are the owner. You are the manager. You are the leader. It's your responsibility.

THE SINGLE BIGGEST DECISION: HIRING YOUR NUMBER TWO

If you want to scale, if you want to actually build something that grows without you getting buried in every single task, you've got to make one of the most important decisions you'll ever make as a business owner—when to hire your number two.

It's the single biggest decision in your business. Period.

Because here's the reality: You can't be involved in everything forever. You need to be in sales. You need to be driving marketing. You need to be focused on revenue and growth. But if you're trying to scale from $3 million to $5 million, or from $5 million to $10 million, you don't have time to be buried in operations. That's where your number two comes in.

I'll be honest . . . it took me a lot of years (and a lot of mistakes) to get this right. I burned through people I thought were my number two. They weren't. I trusted the wrong people early on. But today, I've had my true number two in place for seven and a half years. And that single decision has changed everything for me.

Why? Because I invested in him as a person. I didn't just hire him to take stuff off my plate. I took the time to actually understand what mattered to him.

His church. His high school, where he still does video work and photography for their sports teams. His teaching. His faith. His family. His ability to travel and give back.

Those things are more important to him than my business, and I respect that. Because I've given him the flexibility, the income, and the freedom to pursue the things that matter most to him, I get his full attention when he's here.

That kind of loyalty, that kind of trust . . . you don't buy it. You build it.

And because of that, we've tripled income. We've scaled. And, more importantly, I've been able to focus on what I'm great at, because I finally had someone I could trust to run the day-to-day. Without that number two, you will never break through the ceiling you're sitting under right now.

TWO EXTRA STEPS IN ACTION

While your competition:

- Avoids responsibility and points fingers when things go wrong
- Rules through fear instead of building real loyalty
- Hires employees they barely know and burns through staff
- Stays buried in daily operations instead of focusing on growth
- Delays hiring a true second-in-command because they're afraid to let go

You will:

- Take full ownership for everything that happens inside your business
- Absorb the blame when necessary, but hold your team accountable with high standards
- Build trust, loyalty, and retention by investing in your people as human beings

- Lead from the front—first in, last out, fully engaged
- Hire and empower a number two who allows you to scale while staying focused on what you do best

This is how you separate yourself as a leader. This is how you build the kind of team that follows you through good times and bad. This is how you create a business that doesn't just operate—it grows, compounds, and multiplies.

Chapter 13

ADJUSTING YOUR PLAN

Every business—I don't care if you're just starting or you're doing $20 million a year—will hit a pivotal moment. And usually, you'll hit it more than once. You reach a fork in the road where you either stay the course or you adapt.

Sometimes the pivot is small. Sometimes it's massive. But if you hesitate or refuse to pivot, someone else will pass you. That's how you get disrupted.

Look at what happened to the taxi and limo industries when Uber and Lyft showed up. They didn't innovate. They didn't adjust. They sat around complaining that it wasn't fair, that these companies were skirting regulations. Meanwhile, Uber built an experience customers actually wanted. And they ate everyone's lunch. The companies that adapted—the few that built their own apps, updated their systems, changed their pricing—survived. The ones that didn't? Slow death.

That's why you have to keep your head up. You have to stay humble enough to see the shifts early, and nimble enough to act when the time comes. The marketplace doesn't care how long you've been in business. It only cares how well you serve the customer right now.

The pivot moments are where the 99% freeze. If you want to be in the 1%, you take the Two Extra Steps and you move.

RECOGNIZING WHEN YOU NEED TO PIVOT

Very few businesses finish where they started. That's just reality. The market keeps moving. The world keeps changing. And if you don't change with it, you get left behind.

We just lived through one of the biggest pivot tests in modern business: COVID. Entire industries had to flip overnight.

- Offices shut down and moved to remote work.
- Management structures changed.
- Companies had to learn how to manage and lead teams spread out all over the country. Now many are trying to bring employees back and facing a whole new round of resistance.

The world didn't just snap back. Customer expectations, employee priorities, and buying habits shifted permanently. And businesses who couldn't adapt are still paying the price.

HOW TO SPOT YOUR PIVOT SIGNALS

The faster that you can identify the trends that are happening in the world, in business, the better positioned you'll be. This could be any of a multitude of things that we as the owner, the CEO, need to understand.

1. CUSTOMER BEHAVIOR SHIFTS

Start by watching your customer. How they buy. Where they buy. When they buy.

Just walk through your local mall. If you remember what that looked like before 2019 and compare it to today, you'll see it immediately:

- Entire stores and brands gone.
- Lower foot traffic, even on weekends.
- Shoppers more comfortable buying online than walking through aisles.

Retail isn't dead. But it's been forced to adapt. The ones that invested early in e-commerce are thriving. The ones who didn't are struggling to stay alive.

Same thing with restaurants:

- Quick service and takeout exploded.
- Delivery apps became the norm.
- Dine-in traffic still hasn't fully recovered in some markets.

Look at the big numbers: Amazon exploded. Walmart pivoted hard into online sales. Customer behavior permanently changed.

If you're not watching your customer behavior like this in your own business, you're missing the early warning signs.

2. REVENUE STAGNATION

Here's the other big signal: Your revenue flatlines. You stop growing. You plateau. And most owners convince themselves to "just stay the course."

That's the danger zone.

Because many times, the answer isn't a full reinvention. It's not blowing up your entire business model. Sometimes you just need to pivot small:

- Add an upsell.
- Layer in a new vertical offer.

- Introduce a new service.
- Adjust your pricing elasticity.

Small pivots compound fast if you're paying attention. But you've got to be willing to analyze it, stay objective, and take action while you still have momentum.

THE EVERY-SIX-MONTHS RULE

This is exactly why I run my grader every six months in every business I own. Twice a year, I sit down and run a full analysis. I'm looking at two things:

- My own company's current reality
- My competitors and what's changing around me

Because here's the deal: If sales are flattening, if profit margins are slipping, if new competitors are entering the market—I need to know that fast. I can't afford to drift for 12 or 18 months before realizing I missed a shift.

THE MARKETPLACE WILL ALWAYS TELL YOU

One of the biggest traps we fall into as entrepreneurs is being too busy inside the business to pay attention to what's happening outside of it. Between personal life, employees, sales, fires to put out—you stop watching the market.

But the marketplace is always talking to you. It's giving you clues constantly. If you're paying attention, it'll tell you when you need to pivot. And most of the time, it's not going to be something massive like COVID. It's small shifts you need to catch early:

- Demand changes
- Pricing pressures
- Customer needs evolving
- New competitors showing up
- Technology changing how people buy
- New acquisition channels opening up

Those are your signals. And you better be paying close attention to them.

THE COMPETITOR ANALYSIS PROCESS

This is why every six months you need to run your competitor analysis right alongside your own grader. Start with your usual three to five core competitors—the ones you're always up against. But then widen the lens. You've got to start thinking the way your customer thinks.

It's not just burger joint vs. burger joint. It's Chipotle vs. Blaze Pizza vs. Chopt Creative Salad vs. Panera. Because your customer is simply deciding: "Where am I spending my $15 today?"

- Mexican or pizza?
- Healthy or fast?
- Price-driven or quality-driven?

They're all competing for the same wallet share whether the product is identical or not. And if you're not looking at it that way, you're missing the full picture of your market.

PRICE POINT ANALYSIS

Pricing becomes part of that customer decision tree. Look at it from the buyer's seat:

- Chopt charges $14 for a salad.
- Chipotle gives me a bowl for $9.99.
- If I'm price-sensitive, I go to Chipotle.
- If I care more about the healthier option and I've got the margin to spend, I'll go to Chopt.

Understanding these buyer behaviors is exactly why you run this process every six months. Because sometimes it's not your product that needs to change. It's your positioning. It's your buyer persona. It's your go-to-market strategy that needs to shift.

SMALL PIVOTS, BIG IMPACT

A pivot doesn't mean blowing everything up. Many times, it's a small shift:

- Add-on products
- Upsells
- Service layers
- Targeting a slightly different customer

But if you're not analyzing, you won't see the pivot until it's too late.

THE ULTIMATE PIVOT: EXTRACTING LARGER WALLET SHARE

One of the biggest pivots that changed how I scale companies wasn't about chasing new customers—it was about getting more out of the ones I already had. A mentor of mine, John Boyan (who ran sales at Comdata), drilled this into me years ago.

He said: "It's six times cheaper to extract a larger share of a current customer's wallet than it is to acquire a new one."

Most business owners hear that stat and nod their heads. But they don't actually change their behavior. They stay obsessed with new leads, new sales, new clients. Meanwhile, they're sitting on a gold mine inside their existing customer base.

Here's the shift: I stopped thinking about client retention as just "keeping people happy" and started focusing on wallet share. How do I create more opportunities to serve the same customer at a higher level? How do I stack additional products, services, or upgrades that solve more problems for them?

That's how you create exponential growth without the constant grind of customer acquisition. You don't have to blow up your business model to do it either. Sometimes it's as simple as:

- Adding an upsell or premium tier
- Introducing done-for-you options
- Offering coaching, consulting, or advanced training
- Creating add-on services they'd happily pay for

The beauty is your best customers already trust you. They've bought once, which means they're the easiest people to buy again if you give them a reason.

If you want real scale, stop thinking only about getting more customers. Start thinking about how you can serve the ones you have more deeply. That's where the real leverage lives. That's the ultimate pivot.

TWO EXTRA STEPS IN ACTION

While your competition:

- Stays locked into the same business model even as the market shifts
- Ignores small signals until it's too late to recover

- Focuses only on new customer acquisition instead of maximizing existing customers
- Reacts emotionally instead of analyzing data objectively
- Waits for disruption to hit before making adjustments
- Thinks pivots only happen during major crises like COVID

You will:

- Constantly analyze your business and your market every six months
- Pay attention to shifting customer behavior, pricing trends, and competitor moves
- Make small pivots early that compound into big results
- Adapt your positioning and buyer persona as your market evolves
- Extract more wallet share from your current customer base while still acquiring new ones
- Stay nimble, objective, and proactive so you never get blindsided

This is how you stay ahead. Because while most business owners freeze or fall asleep at the wheel, you'll keep adjusting your plan, stacking advantages, and pulling away from the pack. That's how you build a business that doesn't just survive disruption. It thrives through it.

Chapter 14

START WITH THE END IN MIND

Here's what separates the top 0.1% from everyone else: They don't chase money. They architect outcomes. They don't just build businesses. They build integrated lives where their financial life, personal life, and business life all work together to create exponential results.

While most entrepreneurs are out there scrambling, chasing the next dollar, jumping at every new opportunity, the ones who actually win are playing a very different game. They have clarity. They have structure. They know exactly where they're going, and every decision they make moves them closer to that end game.

This is where 2 + 2 starts equaling 5.

You didn't build your business just to build a business. You built it to fund your life. You built it to create freedom, options, and the ability to actually enjoy what matters most. The problem is, most entrepreneurs never actually define what that life looks like. They build a successful business, but never build a successful life.

A ROOM FULL OF "HIGH PERFORMERS"

In 2015, I was recruited to join an organization called EO—Entrepreneurs' Organization. I got invited to a luncheon at The Palm steak house in downtown Nashville with probably 40 or 50 members and prospects in the room that day.

Great presentations. Really motivating. But here's what stood out to me right away: This wasn't a room of wantrepreneurs. You had to have a business doing at least a million dollars a year just to be considered. These were real business owners who were already doing it.

I ended up joining and got placed into a forum group of eight members. We'd meet once a month, usually for about four hours, sometimes longer if we stayed for dinner after. It was a serious time commitment, but I was all in.

For the first meeting, they told us to come fully prepared—business plan, financials, goals, the whole thing. So I spent hours getting everything together. After all, I didn't want to be the guy who showed up and looked like an idiot. I walked in that first day, and out of the eight people, I'd say I was probably the third most prepared. And honestly, that felt like a win. I wasn't dead last.

Fast-forward six months, though, and a pattern started to show up.

The same three guys, myself included, came prepared every single month. Financials dialed in. Goals updated. We were putting in the work and taking the Two Extra Steps. The other five? They'd stroll in late, no numbers, no real prep, just kind of hanging out. They were good guys, still friendly acquaintances to this day, but they weren't serious. They weren't really running their businesses. They were just reacting.

And after a while, that got frustrating.

So the three of us decided to spin off. We created our own small group called Spark. We brought in a couple of other people who were wired like us. And most importantly, that's where I met a guy who changed the game for me: John Bair.

THE LIFE PLAN THAT CHANGES EVERYTHING

Here's what's wild looking back on it.

All of us in that Spark group were the high performers. We were the ones showing up. We were hitting our numbers, growing our businesses, doing everything that from the outside looked like success. The Type A entrepreneurs. The driven ones who check every box and still feel like we're behind.

But that's exactly why what I'm about to share with you matters so much.

Because you can do all of that right. You can build the business, drive the revenue, grow the team, even hit the financial goals. And still be missing the most important piece. The part nobody really teaches you when you are head-down chasing growth.

That's where John Bair changed the game for me.

John had already been where we were all trying to go. He was a multiple-time CEO who had built companies, sold companies, and gone through the fires we hadn't faced yet. And when he sat us down, he said something that flipped a switch for me.

"Bill, you've got a business plan. But you don't have a life plan."

At first I kind of brushed it off, like most entrepreneurs would. I figured, I'm providing for my family, I'm building businesses—isn't that the plan?

Nope.

That's when he laid it out for me. He said most entrepreneurs make decisions based on one thing. Usually it's providing for the family. Paying the bills. Growing income. But there's no real integration. The business is pulling in one direction. The personal life is pulling in another. The finances are getting duct-taped together somewhere in the middle.

And that's why so many people struggle even when it looks like they're winning.

What John showed me was simple. You don't want separation. You don't want balance. You want alignment. You want to merge three parts of your life together so they actually serve each other instead of competing against each other.

THE THREE-LIFE INTEGRATION

Here's what John taught me. You need to integrate three parts of your life:

- Your financial life
- Your personal life
- Your business life

When you pull all three together instead of trying to balance them separately, that's where exponential results start happening. That's taking the Two Extra Steps to the next level.

And listen, especially if you're an entrepreneur, this whole idea of "work-life balance" is kind of a myth anyway. It's not about trying to keep work and life separate like church and state. That's where most people get frustrated. You're constantly trying to pull time from one to give to the other, and nobody wins.

What John taught me, and what took me a long time to really understand, is you want to mold work and life together. You want your business to fund the life you want, and your life to fuel the business you're building. When you get those two feeding each other, that's where it starts to compound in your favor.

BALANCING AMBITION AND LIFESTYLE

I wish I had understood this earlier because I learned the hard way. Like most entrepreneurs, in my 20s and 30s, I lived in my business. My wife will tell you . . . I went five and a half years without a single vacation. Seven days a week. No exaggeration.

I told myself I was doing it for my family. But the reality? I sacrificed:

- My health
- My marriage
- My relationship with my daughter
- Every ounce of energy I had—all on the altar of ambition

My intentions were good, but it didn't matter. The outcome wasn't aligned. It wasn't what my wife wanted. It wasn't what my daughter would've wanted if she could've said it.

This is why you need to define what success actually looks like, because if you don't, your business will define it for you. And you won't like the cost.

DEFINING YOUR OWN SUCCESS

The cool thing is you get to define your own success. I think a lot of us get hunkered into the white picket fence American dream. We get drawn into the Al Bundy retirement plan where you sit on the couch with your hand down your pants, watching TV all day. That's not success.

And that's certainly not for me.

I will most likely continue to work until the day that I die. I will continue to snowboard and ski and fly-fish and boat on the lake and hike and play golf and do all the things that I love to do with my wife and with my daughters until my final breath.

The ability to mold those together with my businesses is success.

It means turning passions into revenue streams—hosting mastermind retreats in Whitefish, Montana, while spending half my winter on the slopes. It means tax-advantaged structures so travel becomes part of the business plan, not an interruption to it.

That's alignment. That's freedom.

BUILDING WEALTH FOR OTHERS

If your vision ends with you, it's too small. For me, it's never been just about making my family wealthy.

My mission is bigger than that. I want to make my employees wealthy too.

Right now, my goal is simple: turn my two core team members into millionaires. When that happens—and they can sustain it—I'll know I've checked one of the most important boxes on my list. After all, I consider them my family too.

Because that's impact. That's creating opportunities that can change generations for people who have helped me build everything I have.

And it doesn't stop there. It's about preparing my daughters for real life—not just college and careers, but what it actually takes to thrive after school. My youngest is two years away from college. My oldest is already in it, heading for med school. I want them ready for what's coming financially, emotionally, and practically.

It's the same thing I do for my 33,000-person community. Sometimes that means tough love. Most of the time, it means practical advice and frameworks they can put into action immediately.

This is legacy. It's continuing to invest in people, in family, and in the life my wife and I truly want.

MY LIFE PLAN IN ACTION

I snowboarded 43 days last year. My wife did about 20 or 23 days. And we want even more of that. We want to travel to Colorado, Utah, California, Montana—chasing powder for 90 or 100 days every winter once our youngest finishes high school in two years. If I don't intentionally design my business to support that, it'll never happen.

Most people think when you travel, you unplug from work. That's not how we think about it. We want to live that lifestyle while keeping the business running and do it in a way that makes sense financially and from a tax perspective.

That's why this past year:

- I hosted mastermind events at Whitefish, Montana (our home ski resort).
- Ran two couples retreats at the property we own there.
- Hosted a ski and snowboard retreat.

All of that added up to nearly half my days on the mountain, building revenue while living our ideal lifestyle. My wife got to join me for most of it. We made money while doing the thing we love, in the place we love, with the people we enjoy being around.

That's what I want you to see. This is where true integration lives:

- Relationship with your spouse
- Business generating revenue
- Hobbies and lifestyle

All woven together inside your life plan.

THE LIFE EVENT REALITY

Nobody wants to talk about this, but life will punch you in the face. That's not an *if*; it's a *when*. You'll lose people you love. A parent will get sick. A spouse might want to relocate for family reasons. A business partner could bail. Kids will hit phases that demand more of your time. It's not pessimism. It's reality.

Most entrepreneurs build their entire plan as if those things will never happen. Then, when life happens, they scramble. They make emotional decisions in the middle of chaos. They sell businesses under pressure. They burn cash they should have saved. They patch together solutions at the worst possible time—when stress is highest and clarity is lowest.

When my mom passed away eight years ago, I learned this lesson the hard way. We weren't prepared. No systems. No financial plan. No contingency structure. It was chaos—logistically and emotionally. Everything felt harder than it needed to because we had to figure it all out while dealing with grief.

That experience changed me. So, when my father-in-law's health started to decline, we did it differently. We prepared ahead of time.

- **Insurance** was up-to-date and structured correctly.
- **Accounts and property titles** were organized.
- **Bills and subscriptions** were mapped out.
- **Legal documents** were clear and accessible.

So, when the time came, it wasn't easy—but it was manageable. My wife could focus on grieving, not on hunting for paperwork or figuring out financial details.

Life planning isn't just about how much money you want or when you'll retire. It's about protecting the people you love and creating systems that remove unnecessary pain when life inevitably happens.

And it's not just death or illness. It's the moves, the pivots, the surprises you *can* predict if you're honest.

- Your kids might switch schools or need specialized support.
- Your spouse might want to downsize—or upsize—or move closer to family.
- A once-in-a-lifetime business opportunity might require six months of travel.

If you don't anticipate these possibilities, you'll always be reactive. And reactive decisions cost the most—financially, emotionally, and relationally.

I've even seen cultural nuances shape this planning. Two Filipino brothers in my Build STR Wealth mastermind told me they were planning now for the day their parents move in with them. They're designing homes with guest suites and investing in properties that can serve dual purposes—family living now, multigenerational living later. That's smart. That's proactive.

You don't wait until the punch lands. You train for it. That's what these Two Extra Steps are about: thinking how others don't and doing what others won't. So when life changes—and it will—you're not scrambling. You're ready.

FREE LIFE PLAN TRAINING ACCESS

I'm gonna make this super easy for you. Below is a QR code for my full life plan training. This is the exact framework I use for myself and for my clients to stop chasing dollars and start architecting a life that actually works.

It won't take you hours. You can knock the whole thing out in 30–40 minutes. You'll get the workbook. You'll get the process. You'll finally get clear on what you're actually building toward.

And I'll say it one more time because this is where 99% of people miss it: The power isn't in writing some perfect plan. The power is in getting clear and building everything—your business, your family, your freedom—around what matters most.

Start today. Your future self will thank you for taking these Two Extra Steps to create the life plan that 99.9% of entrepreneurs never build.

RULE #1: DO IT SOLO FIRST

You're going to sit down and build your life plan by yourself. No input from your spouse. No discussions ahead of time. You don't do this as a couple. You each do it solo—no influence, no discussions, no nudging each other one way or the other.

Because here's what happens if you don't: One person always ends up driving the conversation. The other person defers. They say, "Yeah, that sounds good," or "I'm fine with that," and you never really get both voices on the table.

You want full honesty. Full vision. No influence. That only happens when you do it separately. So you sit down, work through every section, and write it out exactly how you see it.

RULE #2: MERGE ONLY AFTER YOU'RE BOTH DONE

Once you've both finished your solo plans, now—and only now—you come together and start merging.

Now you can compare what each person wrote. You can see where you align. You can see where you're far apart. And then you have real conversations about how to build a plan that works for both of you.

This is key to make sure nobody gets steamrolled. Nobody gets drowned out. Both people get to fully express what they want before the merge ever happens.

That's why you follow this process. Because if you skip it, somebody's voice always gets lost. And when you're building a plan for your entire future, you don't want anybody sitting there years from now feeling like they never really got what they wanted.

TWO EXTRA STEPS IN ACTION

While your competition:

- Chases revenue with no real end game
- Separates business, personal, and financial lives into competing buckets
- Reacts to life events instead of planning for them
- Builds businesses that trap them instead of free them
- Makes decisions based on short-term income instead of long-term outcomes

You will:

- Architect your business around the life you actually want
- Integrate business, personal, and financial decisions into one unified plan
- Proactively plan for life events before they hit
- Turn personal passions into revenue-generating, tax-advantaged opportunities
- Build freedom, flexibility, and wealth that compounds over decades

You don't just build a business. You build a life where everything works together, feeding each other, creating exponential results that most entrepreneurs will never experience.

Chapter 15

EXIT STRATEGY

One of the biggest reasons I always start with the end in mind, whether that's the revenue goal I want to hit or the exit I want to eventually make, is because most business owners never think about it until it's too late. And when you don't think about it, you're not building a business that's actually sellable.

So what happens when you finally get to the end? You might hit your profit goals. You might hit your revenue targets. But if you didn't build it with an exit in mind, you're sitting on a business that can't really be sold . . . at least not for what it could've been worth.

If you don't have . . .

- Rock-solid books and clean financials
- A scalable model that can run without you
- Clear SOPs (standard operating procedures)
- Documented quality control processes
- A fully staffed and trained management team

. . . then you don't have a sellable asset. You might still find a buyer, but you're going to take a huge haircut on valuation. You'll end up with a much lower multiple on your EBITDA.

For those who aren't familiar, EBITDA stands for earnings before interest, taxes, depreciation, and amortization. That's what most companies use as the basis for your business valuation when you exit.

BUILDING FOR THE EXIT

That's why I start with the exit in mind from day one. For me personally, let's say I want to get to $20 million. I know I need a COO, a GM, and documented processes in every key area:

- Sales
- Marketing
- Customer service
- Production
- Quality control

All of it has to be nailed down so when the time comes, someone can literally walk in, shake hands, grab the keys, and run the business without me.

Now, I'm oversimplifying that a bit. There's usually earn-outs involved, tax strategy, negotiations, and all that. But at the core, this is why I stay laser-focused on the end game. I'm always looking at it from two sides:

- The exit strategy to build a business someone can buy
- The personal goals of what I want to get out of the business while I'm still running it

THE PROBLEM WITH "FIGURING IT OUT"

Most people start a business thinking, *I'll figure it out as I go.* And that's exactly where most of the mistakes happen—because they never stop to actually define what they want out of the business in the first place.

I can't stress this enough: The clarity you get from defining your end game completely changes how you run the business.

It's just like the life plan we talked about earlier. When you have crystal-clear goals, you know where you're trying to land. And that does one really important thing: It lets you reverse engineer every decision. You're not reacting. You're not guessing. You're making stronger, smarter decisions every single day because you know exactly where those decisions are taking you.

GPS FOR YOUR BUSINESS

Without a clear outcome and a clear timeline, you're basically just driving down an open highway with no GPS. You're moving, but you have no real idea where you're headed or how long it's going to take to get there.

When you have that end game locked in, you can:

- Take small, incremental steps
- Know when to turn right or left
- Pause to refuel and recharge
- And still keep moving toward the destination

Most entrepreneurs completely miss this when it comes to their end game. And just to be clear, building for an exit doesn't always mean selling to a third party. The exit might be handing it off to your number two or to a family member. But you still have to build it with that transition in mind. You've got to be ready for it either way.

BUILDING A PREMIUM EXIT-READY BUSINESS

If you own a small business now and you have any inclination of selling in the future, now's the time to take some steps to not only become sellable, but also to go from not sellable to premium exit ready.

What I mean by premium exit ready is to get the highest valuation possible on your business. There are certain factors that come into play for this.

FACTOR #1: ROCK-SOLID SOPS AND TRAINING

If you want to exit your business and not be tied to it after the sale—meaning you don't have to stay on for a year or two as an employee—you need to have bulletproof SOPs and real training systems in place.

I'll give you an example from my own experience. When I started Silver Oak Transportation, everything was in my head. All of it. Chauffeur training, dispatch, reservations, software, DOT compliance, banking, you name it. Sure, I had a few things written down for the drivers, but for the actual operations? Nothing.

Eventually, I hired someone to come in and pull everything out of my head and get it documented. We ended up with a 456-page SOP manual. And you know what? Even that wasn't enough.

MODERN TRAINING REQUIREMENTS

In today's world, it's not enough to just have a big binder of written processes. You need full step-by-step video training for every position inside your company. I'm talking about:

- What happens when the employee pulls in the driveway
- Where they park their car
- How they turn on the lights
- Every single step of their role from start to finish

And honestly, technology makes this easier than ever. I love using Loom videos for this. You record yourself doing the process one time, then you can have that transcribed and turned into written documentation automatically. It's way faster and much more effective than trying to write it all out first.

WHY THIS MATTERS

The reason this is so critical is simple. Whoever buys your company is buying a system they can run without you. If you don't have these SOPs and training systems in place—if you can't show them that this business works without your brain running it—your valuation drops fast.

You might still sell the business, but you won't get the multiple you want. And odds are, you'll end up stuck in the business long after the sale because no one knows how to run it without you.

FACTOR #2: BACK-END FINANCIALS

The second big piece is your back end. And when I say back end, I'm talking about your bookkeeping and accounting.

This is where most small business owners completely screw it up. They don't keep their P&Ls current. They don't keep QuickBooks updated every month. They're what I call "shoebox businesses." They show up to their CPA at tax time with a shoebox full of receipts, and then it takes weeks, and thousands of dollars, for their accountant to sort through it and piece together what actually happened in the business all year.

THE COST OF POOR FINANCIALS

There are two huge problems with this:

1. **Your valuation tanks.**

   If your financials aren't clean and organized, you're going to get a much lower multiple on your EBITDA or gross revenue when you try to sell. Nobody's paying top dollar for a business they can't clearly evaluate.

2. **You don't have the data buyers need.**

   Any serious buyer wants to see your financial performance. Month over month, year to date, year over year—so they can evaluate how the business is actually performing. If you don't have that ready to go, you're dead in the water.

WHAT YOU NEED TO HAVE DIALED IN

At a minimum, your financials need to include:

- QuickBooks (or whatever accounting software you're using) fully updated every single month
- A current balance sheet
- Accurate cash flow reports

And if you're running a service business—whether it's people, vehicles, equipment, or some combination—they're also going to want to evaluate:

- How your employees are being utilized
- How efficiently your assets are being used
- How scalable your service delivery is

If you're not tracking these things, it's very hard for a buyer to understand how your business operates, where the gaps are, and where they can drive more profit after they acquire it.

Bottom line: Clean financials aren't optional if you want top dollar. You need to fall in love with your numbers. The businesses that sell for the highest multiples are the ones that can hand over bulletproof financials on day one.

FACTOR #3: PRICING STRUCTURE AND MARGINS

The third piece is your pricing structure. And this one gets overlooked more than it should.

When a buyer is evaluating your business, they're looking at how your pricing stacks up against their own pricing, and against the market in general. If you've got strong pricing and healthy margins, your business becomes way more attractive. If you don't, it's a problem.

Here's where most owners get stuck: If you don't have a superior product, if you don't have great marketing, if you don't have a real sales engine, the only lever you have left is price. You drop your price to win business. And that might work short-term to keep revenue coming in, but long-term, it crushes your margins.

When margins are thin, buyers lose interest—even if your revenue looks impressive on paper. Because now they have to figure out how to get profitability up. If they're already selling something similar at a higher price point, your lower pricing doesn't help them. It actually complicates things.

Low pricing equals low margin. Low margin equals low multiple. It doesn't matter if you're doing more volume than them. They're looking at profit, not just top-line revenue.

WHERE MOST SMALL BUSINESSES MISS THE BOAT

This right here is where so many small businesses miss it. They get so buried working inside the business that they stop focusing on the two things that actually move the needle:

- Revenue-generating activities to grow the business
- Clean, dialed-in financials on the back end

And when you don't focus on those two things, you never fix your pricing, you never fix your margins, and you end up leaving a ton of money on the table when it's time to exit.

TIMELINE FOR EXIT PREPARATION

If you want to sell five years from now, you need to start getting this dialed in today. If your timeline is two years out, you still need to be locking this in right now—especially the financials on the back end. That part takes time to season.

Most business owners wait too long. They wake up one day and say, "I'm ready to exit." But they haven't done the prep work. And now they've got a mountain of financial cleanup, SOPs to document, and margins to fix. It's overwhelming. In many cases, it's too late to fix everything before the window closes.

You don't want to be trying to backfill years of sloppy books and missing processes while you're in the middle of a sale. That's when buyers start discounting your business, because you've given them reasons to lower your multiple.

The time to prepare for exit isn't when you're ready to exit. It's years earlier.

TWO EXTRA STEPS IN ACTION

While your competition:

- Waits until burnout to think about an exit
- Scrambles with messy books and weak margins
- Keeps everything in their head instead of creating systems
- Builds a business that collapses without them
- Settles for a low-value sale or walks away with nothing

You will:

- Plan your exit years in advance—not in panic mode
- Build clean financials and strong margins from day one
- Create SOPs and video training so the business runs without you
- Position your offer for premium pricing, not a race to the bottom
- Design a business ready to hand off—to a buyer, a number two, or your family

Because when you combine financial clarity, operational systems, and premium positioning, you don't just exit . . . You maximize the value of everything you've built.

Chapter 16

HOW YOU LIVE TWO EXTRA STEPS PERSONALLY

There's no question about it: The grind of running a business can be overwhelming to most. But what needs to happen for you to be able to implement the Two Extra Steps is to identify why you feel overwhelmed as a business owner and get that under control.

That's what I want to walk you through in this chapter, because really, a lot of you are probably reading this and saying, "Bill, I don't have time for that."

Here's the truth: "I don't have time" is the dog-ate-my-homework excuse for adults. That's all it is.

Don't get me wrong. My wife hates when I say that to her, but it's really about priorities and time management. It's about focusing on the things that are gonna move the needle for you and trying to eliminate the things that are not.

I'm not saying just toss them in the trash, but allocate those tasks to a virtual assistant, other employees, or whatever other resources you have inside your business to get them off your plate.

That's what I want to dive into in this chapter. It took me years to be able to really optimize my day-to-day. In 2015, when I started going through my life plan and trying to optimize my life (with the impact that John Bearden had on me and Brea), another component was:

How do I really get more out of my day-to-day so I can focus on the things that are super important?

THE SEVEN-DAY EXERCISE: FINDING YOUR TIME WASTERS

I want you to go grab one of those little three-inch spiral notebooks. Doesn't matter where—7-Eleven, Walgreens, wherever you get your stuff. And I want you to keep that thing with you at all times. Put it in your purse, your suit jacket, your back pocket, whatever you carry. Keep it with you for seven full days.

Now here's what you're going to do: I want you to track every single activity you do, from the moment you wake up in the morning until the time you go to bed at night. Every single thing.

Taking a shower, brushing your teeth, doing a sales call, scrolling Facebook or Instagram, sitting on the couch, watching TV, feeding the dog, helping your kids with homework, going to bed. Every single thing that you do. Every single day.

But I need you to make a commitment to me: Once you write everything down for day number one, do not go back and look at it until you're done with day number seven. You can't look at the previous days moving forward.

When you finish day seven, now you go back and review everything. I want you to go through all seven days three full times. This isn't going to take long—probably 10 to 15 minutes total. But you'll be shocked at what jumps off the page at you.

You'll start to see exactly where your time is leaking. It'll be staring you right in the face.

The aimless scrolling on your phone for an hour. The two-hour TV binge you didn't even realize was happening. The stuff you do automatically that doesn't move the needle one inch.

As you go through and review, I want you to highlight those things that are wasting your time. And write down how much time you're spending on each one. The rule here is simple: If you're doing something at least three times a week, it makes the list.

This is not going to be one page. It's going to take you about two pages per day—sometimes front and back. That's fine. That's exactly what we want.

WEEK TWO: WORK TASKS

Now, once you've gone through the first week and identified all those personal time wasters, we're gonna dial in even more. Week two is about your workday.

Same drill. Grab your notebook. But this time you're only tracking work. Strictly your office time. This could be 6 AM to 10 PM, or it could be 8 AM to 5 PM—whatever your work hours are. You get to set it.

Now start writing down every task you do inside your workday. All the little stuff. All the distractions. All the emails. The meetings. The stuff you keep telling yourself you have to handle personally.

Track every single thing.

Once you finish seven days of work tracking, I promise you, you're going to be blown away by how much junk you're still holding onto that you have absolutely no business doing. You're going to see exactly where you're spending time on tasks that are way below your pay grade. Stuff that you should have delegated to someone else months—or years—ago.

This is where we start creating time. This is where you start reclaiming capacity to actually work on the Two Extra Steps.

YOUR GENIUS ZONE

One of the most important things I ever did was figure out exactly what's inside my genius zone. What I'm actually good at. Like truly, really good at. Not what I can do. What I should be doing.

I am really good at:

- Sales and marketing
- Building community

I am not good at:

- Accounting
- Entering numbers into QuickBooks
- All that back-end financial stuff

So guess what? I don't do it. And I haven't touched it for 20 years.

That's the key right there. You stay inside your lane. You get crystal clear on your genius zone and you spend 95% of your time executing the stuff that lives inside it. That's where your highest value lives. And here's where most business owners screw this up. They don't just waste their own time; they waste their employees' time too.

You've got to figure out your team's genius zones the same way. You've got to make sure your people are spending their time doing what they are really fucking good at. Because if you've got your employees spread across too many things—and they're only spending 20 or 25 or 30% of their time actually working inside their zone of genius—you're wasting your money. You're paying for full-time people to deliver part-time value.

You want to scale a profitable business? You keep yourself and your team locked in the lane where you each create the most value.

THE FOUNDATION: KNOWING YOUR DAILY PRIORITIES

Number one for me is having an understanding of what I want to accomplish every single day before I go to bed the previous night. That is a huge deal for me. If I don't have my next day lined out, I'm already starting behind.

The second thing that I implemented, and I would love for you to implement as well, is to take on the **Warren Buffett methodology of task management**.

THE POCKET NOTEBOOK METHOD

I want you to visualize having that same little pocket notebook from the last time wasters exercise. Open it up and lay it flat on the table in your mind. You have a page on the left and a page on the right.

POCKET NOTEBOOK METHOD

Tasks	Priority
1. Check Email	1. Check Email
2. Client Meeting	
3. Market Research	
4. Update Website	
5. Make Calls	

Left page setup:

- At the very top, in pencil, you write "TASKS" in all caps.
- Below it you label numbers 1, 2, 3, 4 . . .

We all have 50 things that we think we need to accomplish every single day when we wake up. That's why a lot of people have anxiety and feel overwhelmed when they first walk into the office or go downstairs to their basement if they're working from home. But this will simplify it.

So you have 50 things. Numbers 1 through 50. They're all there: number 1, number 2, number 7, 12, 13, 14, 15 . . .

Right page setup:

- You write "PRIORITY" in all caps and underline it.
- You put "Number 1."

Out of those 50 tasks that you have to do today, you pick the most important one. The number one priority. You slide that over to the right-hand side and write it down.

That could be "make your bed." That's the only priority that you have on that right-hand sheet of paper.

HOW IT WORKS IN PRACTICE

Now you shut the notebook. You don't look at the task list again. You're only staring at that one priority. That's what you execute. Start to finish. You don't bounce around. You don't half-complete it. You don't get distracted.

You knock it out. So, in this example, you would get up, you go make your bed, you come back.

When it's done, you open the notebook back up, cross it off your task list, and go right back to work. You pick the next most important task, slide it over, write it on the right side, and repeat.

One task. One priority. Full execution. Then move to the next.

That's how you stay out of overwhelm. That's how you build momentum.

If you do this by priority, really what's happening is you're learning what's the highest priority for you on a daily basis. You're also executing start to finish. Let me say that again: start to finish, one task at a time, one priority at a time.

THE GAME CHANGER: TIME TRACKING

I added one more layer on top of the priority system, and this was a total game changer. This is the Two Extra Steps in action. The part most people don't do, but once you add it, everything else starts to compound.

Every single time I sit down to execute a task, I write down two things:

- The start time
- The end time

That's it. Start. Finish. Two little time stamps. But those two numbers start telling you everything you need to know.

TASK LIST

Task	Start Time	End Time
Task 1	8:30	9:00
Task 2	10:15	11:00
Task 3	1:45	2:30
Task 4	3:30	4:00

Why this matters:

- First, you stop lying to yourself about how long stuff takes. Because we're all guilty of that. We think something's gonna take 10 minutes, but it takes 40. Or we think it's gonna take an hour, but really it's done in 12 minutes. When you track it, you see it. No more guessing.
- Second, once you're tracking it, the pressure changes. There's an accountability that comes when you know you're logging your own time. You don't waste nearly as much. You get in. You get it done. You move on.
- Third, you start building real data. And that's where this becomes powerful. Now you can actually start blocking your calendar in a way that reflects reality. You're not just filling up your day with random appointments. You know how long things take. You can forecast how much you can realistically get done every single day.

This is where I see so many people screw up their calendars. They're just throwing stuff on the schedule like it's all equal. But not every task is equal. Some things take 10 minutes; others take 90. If you're not tracking, you can't plan. And if you can't plan, you constantly feel like you're behind.

For example, think about your team meeting with your staff. Typically an hour-long meeting in most companies. How much of that hour is actually used to its fullest ability and how much is a waste of time? If you can trim that hour-long weekly team meeting down to a 30-minute team meeting and be hyper-focused, that just saved you two hours a month. That's 24 hours a year.

Here's the math:

- If you have 10 people in that meeting, that's 240 hours.
- That is six weeks of work for an employee.
- If you're paying that employee a thousand dollars a week, you just saved $6,000 of wages.

CALENDAR MANAGEMENT: THE THREE-BLOCK SYSTEM

Forget about just being "busy." We're not here to fill time. We're here to execute. This whole system—tracking your tasks, writing down start and stop times—all of it is designed to get you to one thing: real execution.

Because most people aren't actually executing. They're reacting. They're managing chaos. And that's exactly why their task list keeps growing, their anxiety keeps building, and their stress levels keep climbing.

You've got to stop the cycle. And the way you stop it is by taking control of your calendar.

So, once you've gone through your time tracking, once you've eliminated the junk, now we layer in the next piece: your daily execution blocks.

You don't need to go crazy with this. You don't need to be militant. Just start simple.

I want you to schedule at least two blocks every single workday. Or if you're wired like me, you can run three blocks a day. That's how I operate.

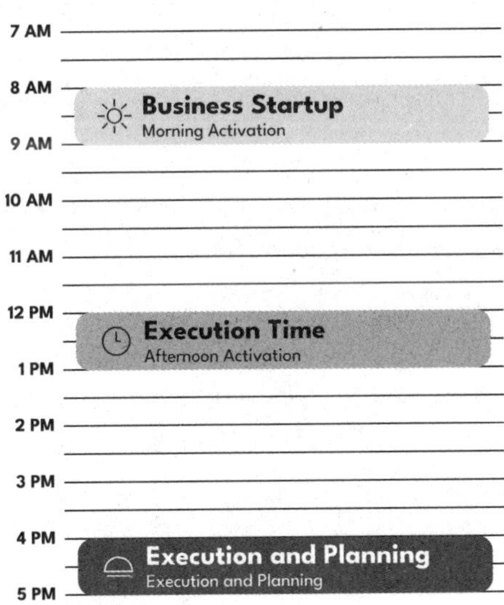

MY THREE DAILY EXECUTION BLOCKS

8 to 9 AM = Business startup (Morning Activation)
Noon to 1 PM = Execution time (Afternoon Activation)
4 to 5 PM = Execution and planning

Note: That noon to one isn't lunchtime for me. That is pure execution time every day.

All three of these times are blocked out. Three hours a day. Multiply that times 5, that's 15 hours a week. That's 60 hours a month that are dedicated purely to execution.

You can just type in "EXECUTION."

During execution blocks:

- No phone calls
- No wasting time on social media
- No checking email
- **EXECUTION ONLY**

WHY THIS WORKS

This is where 99% of people break down. They run their day based on everyone else's priorities. Phone calls coming in, clients texting, staff pulling at them, meetings showing up on the calendar because someone else booked it. They let their day happen to them.

Not me. Not anymore. And not you either.

I start my first block first thing in the morning. Then, if I don't get it all done by 9 AM, I've got my second block waiting for me at noon. Then I close the loop at 4 PM with my third and final block to clean up and prep for tomorrow.

Do I nail it perfectly every single day? No. Life happens. But 80 to 90% of the time, I'm hitting those windows. And that's why my task list stays under control, my anxiety stays down, and my productivity stays high.

If you want to finally stop feeling like you're drowning in tasks every day, this is how you do it. You schedule time to execute.

Because if you don't make time to execute, your calendar will eat you alive. And that's when everything else starts slipping through your fingers.

This system flips it. It puts you back in control of your day.

MAXIMIZING YOUR AVAILABLE TIME

A lot of people hear this system and go, "Bill, if you're blocking your execution windows, you're only wide open from about 9 AM to noon most days. How in the world do you get everything else done?"

Here's the truth: That's plenty of time. Three hours is a lot of time if you're actually focused. That window is where I knock out client calls, staff meetings, one-on-ones, coaching calls, interviews, deep work, research—whatever else needs to be handled that day before I drop back into my next execution block.

The reason it works is simple. I run my calendar like a machine. I schedule everything in 15-minute increments. No wasted motion. No slack built in. I know exactly how long things take because I've tracked it. So, when I sit down to work, I'm not guessing. I'm executing.

THE 20-MINUTE RULE

When somebody wants to do a coaching call with me, I don't default to an hour. I say, "You got 20 minutes, and you better be prepared. Send me an email with all your questions ahead of time so I can prepare, I can research."

And you know what? We're not burning two or three minutes up front with chitchat. We're not wasting five minutes on small talk. We're getting straight to it so I can maximize delivery for you.

The payoff: If I can maximize delivery, that gives me more time at home, gives me more time with my kids, more time to fish and snowboard and do the things that I love, and to take those Two Extra Steps.

WHAT HAPPENS DURING EXECUTION TIME

Inside those execution blocks, it's not complicated. I'm writing emails. Reviewing numbers. Sending proposals. Building content. Catching up on financials. Mapping out the next move. That's where the real work happens.

And the results? They're crystal clear:

- The task list starts shrinking.
- The stress starts dropping.
- The anxiety gets cut in half.
- Your productivity doubles or triples.

That's why I built my entire planner system around this. The calendar management, the time tracking, the execution blocks. This is the operating system that gives me control.

Because when you control your time, you control your business. And when you control your business, you control your life. That's how you create space to operate at a higher level, take the Two Extra Steps, and start seeing 2 + 2 actually add up to 5.

MY PROTECTED TIME

This is where the Two Extra Steps live. This is why I protect my early mornings like gold. I'm up at four or five in the morning and nobody's bothering me.

I've got two daughters. My oldest is off at college. My youngest gets up at six. And when she hits that kitchen at six o'clock, that's her time. No mom. No dad. She's running her own little routine in there, getting her stuff done, and I leave her to it.

But here's the key: Before anybody else in my house is even awake, I've already gotten hours of focused, uninterrupted time. No texts. No DMs. No emails. No coaching calls. No meetings. None of the normal chaos that kicks off when that eight o'clock bell rings and the day officially starts.

Because once eight hits, it's game on:

- Instagram DMs
- Email threads
- Team meetings
- Coaching calls
- Client appointments
- Sales calls

All the noise shows up. That's why I lock in my best work first. I carve out the time that works for me.

BUILDING YOUR MORNING FOUNDATION

Now look, before I even hit my first execution block of the day, I've already stacked my personal morning routine. And I put that on my calendar. Locked in, nonnegotiable.

These three execution blocks we've been talking about? You can drop those anywhere in your day that works for you. For me, though? The real foundation starts first thing in the morning.

MY MORNING ROUTINE GOAL

My goal is simple. I want my entire morning routine finished and complete before 7 AM, every single day.

- Get up
- Brush my teeth
- Take my supplements
- Work out
- Sauna

- Red light therapy
- Shower
- Fully dressed, ready to go

By 7 AM, I've already stacked multiple wins and taken care of my body, my mind, and my headspace. And now I've got margin to engage with my family before the rest of the world comes flying in.

I'm an early riser by default. You don't have to be. If your best work happens at noon, great. If your schedule starts at 10 AM, fine. You can build this around your clock.

WHY THE EARLY START WORKS

The advantage for me is simple. By getting up before my family, I knock all this stuff out while the world is still asleep. Nobody's blowing up my phone. I'm not scrolling email before I even get out of bed like most people do. That phone doesn't get touched until after 8 AM. That's protected time.

By the time seven o'clock rolls around, I'm free to take my daughter to school, help with breakfast, connect with her. That's time I wouldn't have if I was still scrambling to get my own stuff done. I've bought back time before most people even wake up.

CUSTOMIZE THIS FRAMEWORK

You've got to build this to fit your life. Your schedule might look different from mine. That's fine. But the process doesn't change.

- Track your tasks for seven days.
- Identify the time wasters.
- Prioritize your real work.

- Build your execution blocks.
- Lock in your protected time.

One task at a time. Start and complete. Start and complete. And track every single one.

TWO EXTRA STEPS IN ACTION

While most entrepreneurs:

- Stay buried in tasks that don't move the needle
- Waste hours every week on low-value work
- Operate without any real system for prioritizing and executing
- Let their calendar control them instead of controlling their calendar
- Struggle with overwhelm, scattered focus, and growing anxiety

You will:

- Build total clarity on where your time actually goes
- Eliminate the low-value tasks that drain your day
- Lock into your Genius Zone and spend 95% of your time where you drive the most impact
- Execute with discipline, one priority at a time, start to finish
- Track your time and use data to optimize your calendar for maximum productivity
- Build protected time for strategy, creativity, and the Two Extra Steps that separate you from everyone else
- Reduce your stress, sharpen your focus, and scale your business without sacrificing your life

It's not about doing more. It's about doing the right things, the right way, every single day.

Chapter 17

THE TWO EXTRA STEPS ARE YOUR UNFAIR ADVANTAGE

When I started writing this book, my goal wasn't just to help you make more money. It was to give you a mindset—a way of operating—that works in any business, any market, and any season of life.

The Two Extra Steps aren't a trick or a tactic. They're a decision.

A decision to **think how others don't**—to look deeper, question the defaults, see opportunities where everyone else sees obstacles, and hold yourself to higher standards.

A decision to **do what others won't**—to put in the work after others stop, to prepare when others wing it, to execute at a level most will never touch.

That's the difference between a business that blends in and a business that becomes a category of one. That's the difference between a life that feels like a grind and a life that gives you freedom.

When you choose to go a little further than most are willing to go—when you choose to prepare more, learn more, test more, and refuse "good enough"—that's when everything changes. That's the entire playbook. That's how you separate yourself from the noise. That's how you build a business that lasts and a life you never want to escape from.

And if you ever doubt it, remember Tiger. The story that opened this book wasn't really about golf. It was about life. When everyone else packed up and went home, he stayed on the range. He took the Two Extra Steps. That's why he dominated. That's why he separated.

You have the same choice. Every day. In every decision.

The clock is running. The next move is yours. What will it be?

Acknowledgments

For Brea—Thank you for being with me every step of the way and for pushing me to be a better husband, father, and provider. We have built many successful companies together, but nothing compares to the life we have built together with you as the leader.

For Oaklee and Gentry—You blow my mind every day, as you are so much smarter and better than I ever was at your age. I am completely in awe of what you two have accomplished and can't wait to see how you better the world as adults.

Love, Daddy

About the Author

Bill Faeth is a serial entrepreneur, investor, speaker, and the founder of the #1 short-term rental brand (Build STR Wealth) in the industry, with a track record of building and scaling 37 companies across multiple industries and generating more than $1 billion in lifetime sales. He also birthed the STR Wealth Conference, which is the largest in the industry, and his insights have been featured on Fox, Fox Business, NBC News, Merit Street, and other major media outlets. Beyond business, Bill is a dedicated family man who shares his success with his wife, Brea, and their two amazing daughters, Gentry and Oaklee.